D0576592

Brunschwig

& Fils *Style*

Murray Douglas &
Chippy Irvine

With Special Photography by Alex McLean

Foreword by Albert Hadley

A Bulfinch Press Book
Little, Brown and Company
Boston ⁓ New York ⁓ Toronto ⁓ London

Library of Congress
Cataloging-in-Publication Data
appears on page 195.

First Edition
Third Printing, 1997

Bulfinch Press is an imprint and
trademark of Little, Brown and
Company, Inc. Published
simultaneously in Canada by Little,
Brown & Company (Canada),
Limited

PRINTED IN SINGAPORE

Endpapers: Gloriette plaid taffeta

Page i: Jeannie McKeogh covered this
chair in Brunschwig's *Oatlands*.

Previous page: The window seat of
Eveline and Thomas Peardon's library
is the perfect place to curl up and read.
The banquette is covered with *Fleur
Bleue* tapestry, and the bountiful cush-
ions are of *Hameau* taffeta plaid and
Voison taffeta stripe.

Right: This gentle, feminine Atlanta
living room belongs to designer Ginny
Magher. She selected *Catherine* cotton
print for the sofa, to go with a subdued
Aubusson carpet, combining it with two
club chairs upholstered in Brunschwig's
soft blue *Carsten* check. Trimming on
the skirts are wood tassels hand-glazed
by Eugenia Davis. The tassels on the
silk balloon shades are Brunschwig's
Traviata tassel.

*This book is dedicated
to interior designers all over the world,
for whom Brunschwig evolved,
and without whom Brunschwig would not exist.*

Contents ✌

Foreword 🖋

This is a book about style and beauty, about harmony and imagination, about discipline and determination. It's about a family — and what a family! You'll learn all about it, because Murray and Chippy have painted a bold word-picture with broad, dramatic strokes. Not only am I pleased with their efforts, I am also very proud — proud because I have known both of these ladies for a very long time. We are friends.

How I discovered Brunschwig & Fils professionally is another story. I had worked as a decorator's assistant in Nashville, Tennessee, for a short time before I became a corporal in the 861st Aviation Battalion in 1942. After my military stint I found myself back in Nashville, but I was eager to be in New York. As a country boy I had devoured the pages of magazines such as *House & Garden, House Beautiful, Vogue,* and *Harper's Bazaar.* I knew the ropes — or so I thought!

When I enrolled at the Parsons School of Design for their six-week summer course, it was as much to experience the great city of New York as it was to become scholastically involved. I certainly made time to visit all the glamorous trade showrooms I had only read about. With one exception, I was welcomed with open arms. There was Scala-mandré, Schumacher, Cheney Silks, Johnson and Faulkner, Arthur H. Lee, and Fortuny — even the formidable Rose Cumming admitted me to her mysterious and magical shop! Her manner was cool and aloof, but she was nothing compared to Zelina Brunschwig. I was on the threshold of the Brunschwig & Fils showroom, where I could see, displayed with the utmost style, colors, patterns, and textures of great impact. My curiosity was flaming, but I couldn't get in — I simply didn't have an account! Zelina Brunschwig was right there, running things. She was the visible embodiment of Brunschwig & Fils, in a big way.

This sketch, done by Murray Douglas when she was a student at Parsons, is of a room in the Ca' Rezzonico, a palazzo in Venice.

Mrs. B., as she was affectionately called by the staff, was a woman of great style, chic, and inventiveness. She brought life, light, imagination, and more than a dash of wit to an industry that often takes itself too seriously. The Colonel and Mrs. B. had a magic touch.

I'm so lucky to have known and grown with the Brunschwig family. Murray was a student when I was teaching at the Parsons School. Even then her watercolor renderings of rooms were amazing. Several of her room portraits are included in this book; they are astonishingly beautiful.

The book is charming, informative, and inclusive of the hundreds of people who are responsible for helping to make a long-ago dream a worldwide reality.

Bravo and much love,

Albert Hadley

The Company

I ⤜

"Good Design Is Forever"

What is it about the feeling of certain spaces — a fascinating house, a chic apartment, a handsome executive office, a superb hotel, an evocative room in a museum, the cabin of a glamorous yacht, an admired mansion on a hill — that attracts? Without intruding, both their background and their furnishings impart style. Analyzing the decoration, we realize that the curtains, wall coverings, and furniture are visually satisfying yet relaxed, fresh but familiarly rooted in tradition. Even the plain fabrics are rich and subtly textured. Wallpapers add dimension — height, architectural detail — or invite an emotional response, a feeling of well-being. Patterned textiles are refined yet colorful. Upholstered furniture is more than merely comfortable and inviting: the design on a printed cloth works properly on a chair; the anchoring braids and fringed edgings add genuine but unostentatious panache.

All these elements are an integral part of the Brunschwig & Fils mystique. No other company is as renowned for its vast array of wonderful designs — over seventeen thousand fabrics and wall coverings. With the recent surge of interest in decoration, there is a need to tell the vibrant story of this influential company, from its founding a hundred years ago to its current growth on the world scene. The second part of this book presents the Brunschwig design aesthetic at work in a series of interiors by many different designers. The name Brunschwig & Fils is familiar to many from its luxurious advertisements, which appear in all the major shelter magazines. For those who know good design, the name Brunschwig & Fils is to decorative fabrics what Chippendale is to chairs or Rolls Royce is to cars.

Today Brunschwig's corporate headquarters is in North White Plains, New York. But the firm's true inspiration begins in France, where Achille Brunschwig started his company. Good design has been at the firm's heart and soul from the beginning, and each generation of

Opposite: Damasks are not only silky — they can also look quite modern, as does this cotton and viscose *Fourvière* damask from Italy, used by New York designer Juan Montoya on an Art Deco chair.

Previous page: Though represented in England for many years, since 1990 Brunschwig & Fils has had its own showroom in London, at the design center at Chelsea Harbour. Outside the window can be seen the distinctive taxicabs of London. This is one of the many Brunschwig offices throughout the world.

the family acknowledges that French style — in décor, fashion, design, color, and the arts of living — has been paramount for centuries. "We are essentially a French house," says Senior Vice President Mrs. Murray B. Douglas, niece of Mrs. Zelina Brunschwig. The French design spirit takes its ideas from whatever culture it finds intriguing. The French borrowed from China and called it chinoiserie; they borrowed from Japan and called it japonaiserie; they borrowed from England and called it *Le Style Anglais*. But they made all these styles uniquely French, always with a tremendous sense of proportion, balance, and elegance. To translate this spirit for today's taste, in America and around the world, is what Brunschwig & Fils tries to do.

Decorative Influences 🖋

Inspired by the Brunschwig & Fils motto, "Good Design Is Forever," Murray Douglas gives lectures to student designers and collectors all over the United States and abroad. In many of her extensively researched slide shows she surveys the history of decorative design and crafts from the seventeenth century to the present. Woven fabrics have been used for thousands of years (a July 1993 article in the *New York Times* described the discovery of a nine-thousand-year-old piece of linen). Fabric has been used to decorate interiors for centuries. Patterns formed by weaving have ranged from basic over-and-under tabby weaves, like palm mats, to complex brocaded designs imitating embroidery.

In seventeenth-century Europe, when the Low Countries prospered from overseas trade, wealth was displayed by elaborate clothing and the use of rich tapestries — sometimes gilded leather — as wall coverings. Decorative rugs too precious for the floor were displayed on tables. In England and France such tapestries were not merely symbols of wealth, but also practical insulators in houses heated only by the fireplace. Windows were expensive and therefore small, so tapestries provided a decorative, scenic way to open up a room. Window curtains were not as important as the often elaborate hangings used around beds for warmth and protection from the bad night air. The furniture was often covered in the same fabric as the hangings (an arrangement known to upholsterers of the time as en suite, though that term is also used nowadays to refer to adjoining rooms). Textiles were plain, embossed, or embroidered wool or silk damask, and they were often decorated with contrasting trimming. Contemporary inventories of the period reveal that bed hangings and tapestries were the most esteemed

The epitome of French style is revealed in this François Boucher scene of a young woman and her maid (*La Toilette*, 1742), from the Thyssen-Bornemisza collection, now in Madrid. The walls and chair are covered en suite with a damask design. The presence of the Chinese screen indicates that among the well-to-do Eastern design was influencing Europe.

of all furnishings, handed down from one generation to the next. Most early window curtains have disappeared, ravaged over the years by light. Twentieth-century research shows that not only in Europe but all down the east coast in colonial America, wool was commonly used in furnishings. Most of these original fabrics have disappeared as well, eaten away by moths.

The European aristocracy and royalty — especially in France — continued to support and encourage skilled weavers in the eighteenth century, subsidizing any trade involved with textile making. Paintings of the time show glorious boiseries; exquisite silk damask–upholstered suites of furniture; gentlemen arrayed like peacocks in embroidered waistcoats and underwaistcoats; Genoese and embossed velvet on the walls; mirrors, gilt, and candlelight picking up color, contrast, and brilliance. All these stylish adornments kept many trades occupied. Meanwhile, new, exotic, and highly desirable furnishings and clothing textiles were being welcomed from India, China, and the Middle East. Even then Parisians liked to be at the forefront of fashion.

Louis XIV's great palace at Versailles was the Sun King's showplace, representing the height of French design in the late seventeenth and continuing all through the eighteenth century. The palace's enfilades of rooms imparted splendor, scale, light, and magnificent presentation. The reigns of Louis XV and Louis XVI saw decorative changes

For this bedroom, New York designer Charlotte Moss used Brunschwig's adaptation of the botanical print *Dr. Thornton's Tulips*, from the doctor's *Temple of Flora* folio.

that reflected the styles of their era, impressing us even now with their grandeur. Murray Douglas remembers touring the palace with curator Gérald van der Kemp — a tall Dutchman with a French spirit who cared passionately about Versailles. She was taken behind the boiseries of Marie Antoinette's bedchamber and allowed to enter the room by a tiny door right beside the formal, very grand bed with its baldachin to the ceiling. Less privileged tourists, standing beyond the barrier at the foot of the bed separating the public from the room, gasped as she appeared. "For one brief second," says Mrs. Douglas, "I felt like Marie Antoinette. But I kept my head."

The influence of the Directoire and of Napoléon brought style changes of a more sober, masculine nature. Military themes dear to the Emperor's heart — tented ceilings, classic drapery — changed the way fabrics were used in decoration. During the Napoleonic period lots of stripes and borders and Roman, Greek, and Egyptian motifs showed up.

Fabric designs reflected the growing European interest in botany from the late eighteenth century on. Ideas were borrowed from many sources. Plants were being imported from all over the world, and artists who faithfully rendered illustrations for books on flora and fauna also

Coraux, an unpretentious early-nineteenth-century documentary print from the Musée des Arts Décoratifs, works well even in a grandiose room such as this large-proportioned bedroom. Its "state bed" was designed by Edward Springs for the 1988 Duke Mansion Showhouse in Charlotte, North Carolina.

engraved designs for textiles. Between 1799 and 1807 an English physician interested in botanical drawings, Dr. R. J. Thornton, printed his *Temple of Flora* folio. He commissioned a series of botanical sketches to be engraved and hand-colored, but he went bankrupt in the process. He tried to recoup his losses by founding the Royal Botanical Lottery, but when it failed he was reduced to poverty. In 1968 Brunschwig & Fils adapted a design from a 1920s documentary fabric from their archives that had obviously been based on a colored mezzotint of tulips — number 10 — from Thornton's folio. The document had a stripe in the background, which was included in Brunschwig's 1968 glazed chintz version of *Dr. Thornton's Tulips*. The design was reintroduced in 1991 on linen, minus the stripe, demonstrating how an intrinsically sound design goes on and on.

A simple little pattern that came about in the early nineteenth century, when everyone was fascinated by naturalistic biological discoveries, is *Coraux*, a coral pattern adapted from a documentary fabric in the Musée des Arts Décoratifs. Brunschwig & Fils has translated the pattern onto both fabric and wallpaper, in light and dark colors and sometimes with the original pattern's dotted stripe.

The ideal of a mid-twentieth-century decorating style was formulated by Billy Baldwin, who successfully introduced sophistication into the more relaxed, post–World War II attitude. This synthesis was exemplified by the use of cotton in place of silk and brocade, mirror, screens, simple flower arrangements, and new versions of traditional furniture, such as his armless "Billy Baldwin" chairs. The chair covering is *Pique-nique*, a long-lived print used for fabric and wallpaper.

Toward the end of the nineteenth century, rooms were smothered in fabric. Portières hung on doors between rooms, rugs were piled on top of carpets, furniture was deeply tufted and fringed, and grand late-Victorian houses flaunted overpowering swags of drapery. Nature, too, was brought indoors in the form of plants, and every house of importance sprouted a conservatory. In reaction, an aesthetic movement at the end of the century helped clean out the overabundance. Novelist Edith Wharton, who chronicled the lives of the affluent, joined architect Ogden Codman to write a significant — and sensible — book called *The Decoration of Houses*. One woman in particular — the fabled Elsie de Wolfe — helped establish the idea of a professional decorator, a job previously held by architects and upholsterers.

Some fifty years later the American decorator Billy Baldwin spearheaded a fresh, mid-twentieth-century style that was as elegant and classic as the design ideas of the eighteenth century. Much of its effect was achieved by means of textural variations — glossy floors and polished crystal and mirrors set against pared-down flower arrangements, and an increasing use of well-designed, unpretentious cotton fabrics on simple furniture.

French Decorative-Fabric Traditions

The French are protective of their design traditions. One wing of the Louvre — the magnificent palace in Paris used by French kings before Louis XIV built his palace at Versailles — houses the Musée des Arts Décoratifs. This museum was where Mrs. Brunschwig (née Zelina de Maclot Comegys and known to many as Mrs. B.), a dynamic forward-thinking American, studied and sketched in the 1920s while attending the Parsons School of Design's French division in the Place des Vosges.

When Murray Douglas in turn went to Paris as a Parsons's student, she heeded the words of her formidable aunt: "If you want to understand the progression of French style, go to the Musée des Arts Décoratifs and study their lineup of chairs, which starts at Louis XII and goes all the way to Art Moderne."

The recently refurbished museum displays rooms decorated with the best of their various periods. As Mrs. B. did before her, Murray Douglas sketched in France's great museums, learning that there is no better training for the eye than to put on paper what you see, embedding taste, style, and proportion into the consciousness. Mrs. Douglas often says, "If you see good things from the very beginning, bad imitations stick out like a sore thumb; that's why, at Parsons, we had to measure and draw furniture, putting it in our heads and in our notebooks."

The Brunschwig Archive and Library ✎

Mrs. B. had collected documentary textile designs found in American houses for years, and she was keen to make use of the great collection of European documentary patterns that her husband, Colonel Brunschwig, and his father, Achille, had collected and stored in France. It was arranged for these precious documents to be packed in map cases and sent to America for safekeeping during World War II. More than ten thousand documents are now in the well-designed, efficient archives at the Brunschwig & Fils New York office, currently under the direction of full-time archivist, Judith Straeten. New documents and books are continually added. The Brunschwig & Fils collection displays a constant recycling of past designs — updated and recolored when necessary — illustrating the company's motto that good design really *is* forever.

The Brunschwig archives are one of the firm's great strengths. New original designs are recorded on two photographs; one copy stays in the archives, and the other goes to the huge Brunschwig & Fils warehouse and headquarters in North White Plains — an expedient move in case of accidents such as fire. The firm is always on the lookout for new designs, adapting them not only from antique textiles and artists' renderings but also from vintage articles such as hatboxes, attic wall-

Archivist Judith Straeten organizes Brunschwig's collection of documentary fabrics and wallpapers in the company's sleek and practical repository, complete with its own climate-control panel.

One of Brunschwig's wallpapers, "Lunéville plates," depicts the early eighteenth-century decorative conceit of plates displayed on the wall.

Opposite: Fabrics fill the shelves in Brunschwig's warehouse in North White Plains, N.Y.

paper scraps, old costumes, and fragments of scarves. Some of the earliest documentary patterns in the archives came from ecclesiastical robes whose patterns were not only intended for church use but also exemplified the best and most beautiful embroidery and weaving of their day. Whether a scrap of seventeenth-century embroidery or an early-nineteenth-century glazed-wool brocaded cloth, these ideas are translated into printed chintz, woven cloth, and, since the 1960s, wallpaper. In each case, Brunschwig & Fils tries not to change the scale of the pattern, knowing that this is often the reason the pattern works so well.

The Design Studio ⟿

A second strength is Brunschwig's New York design studio. Its clear north light is the envy of visiting European suppliers. Here documents that may be little more than fragments are painstakingly interpreted into suitable repeating patterns for printing. Different colorways are designed for each pattern, though the occasional pattern turns up — such as realistic flowers ("We won't do blue roses!" says Murray Douglas) — that only works well in one color. "I like the idea that the director of the studio is an artist who paints," says Mrs. Douglas, who was director herself for many years. "Directors can help their colorists so much more if they themselves have the experience of seeing with a brush."

Printing Mills ⟿

One reason Brunschwig & Fils has succeeded for so long is because Colonel Brunschwig and his family established steadfast relationships with many of the great French mills early in the firm's history. One such mill is Manufacture d'Impression sur Etoffes (MIE), at Ribeauvillé, in Alsace. MIE is now a modernized, busy mill; it was already printing cloth in the eighteenth century, at the time when renowned textile innovator Christophe-Philippe Oberkampf was printing his brilliantly chic indiennes in Jouy-en-Josas, near Versailles. On the top floor of the Ribeauvillé mill, traditional block printing is done by hand, much as it was then. This is a laborious business. The hardwood block, which has a design carved or engraved into its face, has holes for the fingers — like a bowling ball — on its back, so the printer can lift it and charge it with pigment. The dye pad is on rollers and moves with the printer along the table. He places the block on the cloth, matching it up with tiny protruding pins, and then taps it lightly with a wooden mallet to force the dye onto the cloth. As many as eight colors are required in every repeat, each one requiring a separate block. This is the slowest method of printing because it is all done by hand, but subtle effects are produced that can be achieved no other way.

On the floor below is the hand-screen-printing atelier. The screens — large, traylike objects — require two men to lift and to place in position along sixty-yard-long tables. Repeats are printed alternately, giving the dye a chance to dry before the missing repeats are printed. Hand screening is a faster process than block printing, but it still takes time. The advantage is that, being a slow process, the dye has a chance to dry before the next color is applied. For instance, blue printed over *dry* yellow produces green; if the yellow were still wet, the green color would be diffused, making it necessary to add an extra screen.

On the next floor down is a mechanized system called flatbed printing. The fabric moves on a belt, while the screens remain stationary — a much quicker process. Even faster is rotary screen printing, in which dye is extruded from inside a drum-shaped screen onto the cloth; as many as twenty-five rotary screens can run at once. Most stripes are printed on rotary screens to provide a smooth, continual line. Rotary and flatbed screens print "wet on wet," however, so a separate screen is required for each color. The dye must be aged as soon as possible because colors often react differently if left overnight. One day's printing is designated a "dye lot" and numbered accordingly. Using the hand block process, about 10 yards can be produced a day; hand screening produces about 125 yards a day; rotary screens can churn out 5000 yards a day. The price of the finished cloth reflects these figures. Rotary screens, though efficient, never achieve the wonderful, shaded effects that can be accomplished by hand screening or the very special nuances that occur with hand block printing. There will always be a place for these distinctive but slow processes, and the customer has to understand and desire them badly enough to pay the price and wait, in rare cases, six months to a year for delivery.

Printing on fabric is a fairly recent process. Hand-painted textiles came to Europe from India in the seventeenth century. European traders, mostly Portuguese at first, brought back these excitingly brilliant and colorful cotton cloths. Europeans were accustomed to woven fabrics — some very elaborate — of linen, wool, and silk, but they used little cotton. Some simple block and resist-dyed prints had been

The first that Americans saw of multi-colored, printed fabrics were *palampores* such as this, usually in spirited tree of life patterns. This version was adapted by Brunschwig & Fils from one at the Royal Ontario Museum in Toronto, Canada. Standing in front of it are Vice President of Development Ross Francis and Associate Director of Prints Marianthi Raptis.

In his Southampton bedroom, New York decorator Kevin McNamara used the definitive French-produced *palampore* design, *Grand Genois*, which is sold in the United States by Brunschwig & Fils.

done in Europe, but the Europeans had seen nothing like these exotic, washable *indiennes*, as the French called them. The first patterns to arrive were in fact rather too exotic for European taste, but traders worked out designs that melded the strange, fanciful Indian flowers with the European love of realism, producing composite designs that still appeal. Cloth often came in the form of coverlets or bedspreads called *palampores*, composed of one huge repeat surrounded by a border, showing the tree of life growing up from the ground and branching out into twigs, leaves, and colorful, imaginary flowers.

Using the Past ≈

Recycling furnishing fabric is not a new idea. In the 1930s, at Colonial Williamsburg, the tall windows of the ballroom in the Governor's Palace were hung with very grand eighteenth-century bordered curtains made from partly worn indiennes. Curtains, no matter how fast the dye, fade sooner or later unless protected from light. This set, of early-eighteenth-century hand-painted Indian cotton, had evidently faded at the edges — the most vulnerable part. They had been refurbished many years later with a fancy border of European-printed, blue and red-ground *indienne*-style fabric, sewn on by hand, with a pale blue ribbon outlining the appliqué. Brunschwig & Fils adapted one of these historic curtains from a later owner, calling the design *Ménars*. Though *Ménars* was produced in fabulous colors, everyone looked at it and, declaring it wonderful, asked, "How can we use it?" Some time later Vincent Fourcade, of Denning & Fourcade, took Mrs. Douglas with him to Thomas de Angelis, one of New York's notable upholsterers, and showed her how he was covering some marvelous sofas for Mrs. Charles Wrightsman's house in Palm Beach. The house was shown in *House & Garden* in a sensational ten-page spread, with back-to-back sofas covered in pale green *Ménars* with a rich blue/red border, enhancing the turquoise Chinese paper already on the wall. But the article did Brunschwig & Fils no good, because there was no mention of the name. "Nobody knew where to get the stuff!" says Murray Douglas. "I begged Vincent Fourcade to upholster a similar chair, and we used it as an advertisement. The sales of *Ménars* just went wild." The method Mr. Fourcade used to cover the furniture is known as railroading, or running fabric sideways on the seats, an effective way of handling an unusual pattern which is often used in contract work. It pays to employ a decorator who has innovative ideas.

In the eighteenth century not only aristocratic French style makers but also the middle class became mad for what the French called *chites* — printed, washable calicoes (which we call chintz, after the Sanskrit word *chitra*). Established silk-mill owners, however, saw these imports as a threat. Printed *indiennes* were banned, but the law was flouted, even though the authorities occasionally tore dresses from women's backs. The modish Madame de Pompadour had her portrait painted by François-Hubert Drouais in 1763, defiantly wearing a dress made of the forbidden fabric. She was the largest stockholder of the Compagnie des Indes — the French equivalent of the East India Company, which imported screens, fans, porcelains, *papiers peints* — the forerunner of wallpaper — as well as fabrics. Gradually the secret processes for fixing the dyes to make them washable were learned, via clandestine methods such as European trade spies disguised as Jesuit priests and smuggled formulas written in invisible ink. The mordants used to fix Indian dyestuffs — involving such unlikely ingredients as

Mr. and Mrs. Wrightsman's house in Palm Beach — now lost to the wrecker's ball — shows Denning & Fourcade's use of *Ménars*, a pattern based on hand-painted seventeenth-century Indian *palampore*. The design was recycled a century later by adding borders of European-printed *indiennes*.

elephant dung and buffalo urine — were eventually duplicated chemically, and European factories were able to print their own *indiennes* on imported cotton, sparking a new and lucrative industry.

A documentary hand-blocked French *indienne* printed by Oberkampf in the late eighteenth century was in the archives of the French firm Braquenié, who reproduced it in the twentieth century. The document the firm had been given was faded, and they reproduced it just that way, with subtle blues and pinks. In the 1980s Brunschwig & Fils came across a pristine, more vividly colored document of the same print which had not been exposed to light. The colors were more radiant, and in addition to a far brighter blue and reddish pink, the design included green and yellow. In the eighteenth century, green could only be obtained by "penciling blue" — hand painting with indigo dye — blue on top of yellow, which always produced a slightly feathered effect. On the faded Braquenié document the yellow — which is prone to be fugitive — had faded and disappeared, leaving only blue. Brunschwig now imports the print to America, calling it *Creil*, after the French town. It is available in either the soft, faded version or the more vibrant original coloring.

Trade with China brought about a passion for chinoiserie, a style that reflected European fantasies of Chinese life — ephemeral pagodas, long-tailed birds, men in coolie hats, soft-colored, flower-laden vines. (The French artist Jean Pillement combined Indian and Chinese themes in a particularly distinctive way.)

The most renowned fabric-printing mill was that of the Swiss family Oberkampf, whose *indiennes* and Chinese-inspired monochrome toiles (and whatever other style became fashionable) made the town of Jouy-en-Josas — strategically chosen just outside Versailles, where the royal and the rich gathered — synonymous with finely printed fabrics.

English and Irish mills had been making one-color printed fabrics with engraved plates similar to *toiles de Jouy* (the latest research points to an Irish mill as being the first, in 1752) or copperplate prints, the original English term for what we now refer to as a toile. English mills began making them in 1755, but the Oberkampf factory did not start producing them until 1770. Their distinctive look was characterized by monotone engravings of realistic, often pastoral scenes that reflected philosopher Jean-Jacques Rousseau's interest in *La Nature*. Provincial country styles became fashionable as design topics as did current events, like the obsession for ballooning depicted in *Le ballon de Gonesse* or American Independence in *La Liberté américaine*. (See

Creil also works well in a simply decorated (in contrast to the grandeur of the French room), very American room such as this, the "Lafayette" bedroom at George Washington's Virginia house, Mount Vernon. Though this room was previously decorated using a monotone toile, a recently discovered letter from Lafayette to his family back in France indicated that he loved the bedroom he stayed in at Mount Vernon because it was decorated with an *indienne* design.

Opposite: The *indienne* print, called *Creil* in America, is shown here in a new color variant. The print was used in this high-style French music room (in the villa at Bagatelle, near Paris) as part of a splendid 1994 exhibit of Braquenié fabrics. (Many of the exhibit's fabrics and trimmings are now available in the United States from Brunschwig & Fils.)

This documentary toile — or copper-plate print, as these patterns were termed in England — was named *Bromley Hall*, after the place in England where it was first printed. (Also see it in use in Chapter 13, p. 151.)

In this sewing room, designed for the 1994 Junior League Showhouse of Boston by Liz Mitchell of Marblehead, Massachusetts, the documentary toile *Bromley Hall* was used to upholster the walls. The border was used on the love seat; the middle cushion is covered in a finely engraved pattern of cups and saucers called *Minton*. The furnishings are a blend of eighteenth- and nineteenth-century high style, and country pieces from America, Europe, and the China trade. The overall effect is elegant yet warm and approachable.

Chapter 6, p. 78, for information on *Dublin Toile*, reproduced from a 1760 design.) One of the best-known designers of toiles was Jean-Baptiste Huet, who produced many genre scenes for Oberkampf. Often rooms were decorated en suite with a *toile de Jouy*. This fresh new look, popular in the late eighteenth and early nineteenth centuries, was used on *everything* — bed hangings, coverlets, furniture, and walls (for in those days, unlike today, no *toile de Jouy* wallpapers were available).

The French, German, Italian, and Swiss mills Brunschwig & Fils now works with are super-clean and up-to-the-minute, efficiently producing magnificent textiles. Brunschwig also depends on a number of English mills that produce quality goods. At Edward Turnbull & Sons, Ltd., in Ramsbottom, Lancashire, a semimechanized Gali machine prints the same pattern simultaneously on two tables of identical length. The two tables virtually race each other, so it's become a custom for workers to place bets on the winner!

At the time this photograph was taken, this master weaver was in his early eighties and had worked for this family-operated mill for more than sixty years. He is weaving a silk- and chenille-brocaded satin for the restoration of the queen's bedroom at the Château de Fontainebleau — a project that is now in its twentieth year.

Weaving Mills 🖋

The old French textile mills — creators of complex and sophisticated silk damasks, brocaded cloth, and velvets — have survived to this day despite the availability of cheaper goods. Creating beautiful fabrics is considered a magnificent craft in France, and many French looms are still operated by hand. Just as aristocrats and royalty once supported these skills, now the French government subsidizes many historic factories. In Lyon and Tours, important centers for silk weaving, you can find mills where one worker, using an original loom, may produce no more than a few centimeters a day of an intricate brocaded silk. Going into these ancient ateliers is like stepping into the past, even though many dedicated young people work in them, learning an ancient craft. The atmosphere is almost spiritual, a far cry from the noisy, mechanized modern factories. Music, if allowed, is classical and subdued. Most mills are quiet, because the weavers like to hear the satisfactory tinkle of the bell that marks the completion of each intricate row.

Brocading — which is a process, not strictly speaking a fabric style — is a laborious business. The figured design has to be inter-

In her New York apartment, Ross Francis's own chair — given to her by Mrs. B. — was reproduced by Brunschwig & Fils and called the *Francis* chair. It is upholstered in *Penelope*, a brocaded linen. The wool yarns look as though they have been embroidered, but they are actually brocaded into the background linen.

woven back into the fabric while the unembellished part of the cloth is kept lightweight — a quality the French find desirable. If the extra weft threads at the back of the design are woven in and carried to the selvedge, thus doubling the weight of the cloth, it is not truly brocaded, but a *lampas*, a heavier and somewhat easier to make fabric (still expensive because of the large amount of silk required).

Complex early looms required several hands to operate. The pattern scheme had to be read by a "drawboy," who was responsible for lifting the "heddles," a device that lifts the warp threads to allow the shuttle to pass the weft — or weaving threads — through the warp, forming the design.

Early in the nineteenth century, Joseph-Marie Jacquard (1752–1834) invented a punch-card attachment that revolutionized weaving.

The invention programmed the pattern and automatically lifted the heddles. Because weavers were terrified of losing jobs, riots broke out all over Europe and Jacquard looms were destroyed. Eventually weavers became used to the new attachment, realizing they could produce cloth much faster and thus more money would be earned for all.

Tales about skilled and seasoned French handweavers are legion. One hears about octogenarians who receive a special sixty-yard order, finish it — knowing it will be their last commission — and quietly die the day after it's shipped. Or one hears about the time the two best weavers of the famous *Tiger* velvet were both hurt in a car accident, and it was six months before manufacture of the cloth could be resumed.

Producing authentic *Tiger* and *Leopard* velvet tests the skill of weavers to the limit. Every design student wants to own a cushion of this luxurious cloth, which now retails at almost two thousand dollars a yard (and is only twenty-five inches wide). Most velvet is constructed face to face, like a sandwich, then slit between to form the pile. *Tiger* velvet is woven single-faced, with a silk pile and a Jacquard pattern to form markings. Between each pass of the shuttle, a slotted wire is inserted to make loops, which will create the pile. After each ten rows, the loops are cut by hand with a blade that fits into the slot; one slip of the knife and all the yardage is ruined. The weft threads are then beaten back to make the fabric tight, and weaving continues. No wonder the price is high. Still, no matter the price, or how many other companies attempt to knock off (trade parlance for copy) the design, Brunschwig's *Tiger* and *Leopard* velvets are steady sellers.

Opposite: For the drawing room of the 1818 Benjamin Phillips House in Charleston, South Carolina, decorator Carol Pelzer designed curtains of French *Moulins* damask. This luxurious silk-and-cotton fabric comes in a range of twenty-six colorways. Ms. Pelzer played off the *bleu/saumon* combination on one side, with beige on the other. The woodwork surrounding the window picks up the subtle coloring, and both combine perfectly with the Chinese wallpaper.

In his own apartment, which he used also as an office, the late New York designer Richard Neas enjoyed the luxury of *Leopard* velvet upholstery on a love seat, with *Tiger* velvet cushions, and a handsome Napoleonic chair made by the cabinetmaker J.-F. Belanger. The Louis XVI chairs with harp motifs, signed Jacob, have black seats of *Salins* horsehair texture. (See Glossary, p. 185, for more about horsehair.) The gilded sunburst mirror is late eighteenth century, from an Italian church.

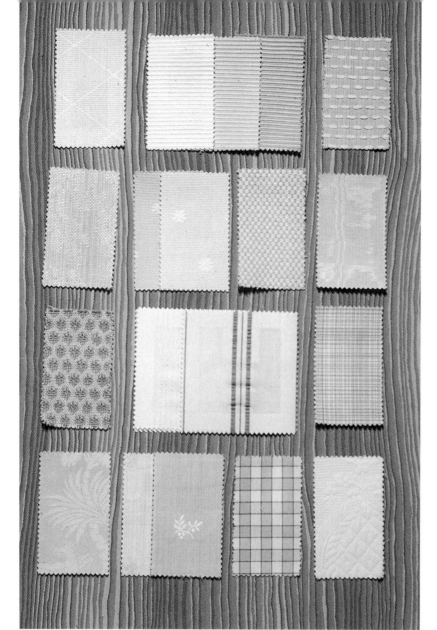

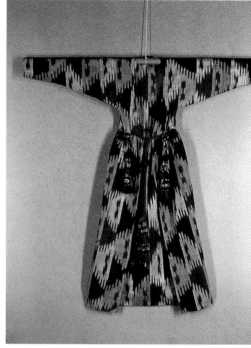

This is an antique garment bought from an Afghan textile dealer in the late 1960s. Brunschwig donated the garment to the Cooper-Hewitt Museum. The design inspired Brunschwig's *Kabul* pattern (shown in a Boston room on p. 100 and in a Minnesota room on p. 110).

Some designers prefer to work primarily with woven textures. Here is a selection of neutral-colored swatches of weaves from the Brunschwig collection, shown against a background of *Teawood* wallpaper.

From the Brunschwig & Fils archives, this *chiné* pattern, *Comtesse d'Artois*, is held together with a fine cobweb of temporary crossthreads while it is awaiting its permanent weft. Above it is a piece of the finished warp-dyed silk.

Other Fabric Techniques 🖋

Embossed textiles, a category of design popular in the seventeenth and eighteenth centuries, were originally intended to imitate woven damasks. The French call the embossing technique *gaufrage* (a *gaufre* is a waffle). The process is similar to that of making waffles, heat-pressing a pattern onto cloth such as wool or velvet. Nowadays it is often less expensive to reproduce a gaufrage using a Jacquard-patterned weave, rather than creating the rollers needed for embossing. With time some of these fabrics develop a *ton-sur-ton* effect, because the surface that is not pressed down darkens with age while the lower, compacted area remains truer to the original color.

Moreen is a vintage textile Brunschwig & Fils produces on special order for both historic and contemporary house furnishings. A plain wool weave, it is constructed with a heavier weft thread that produces a subdued rib. This allows the fabric to be embossed with a pattern or moiréd for a watered effect.

Warp printing produces a particularly distinctive type of pattern. As the name implies, the warp threads — held by a spiderweb of weft threads — are printed first and then put on the loom, where the real weft threads are added to soften, mute, and subtly alter the look of the design. The process produces a printed effect, yet the fabric is the same on both sides. Although the technique started in the Middle East, where the textiles produced were called *ikats*, warp printing was also practiced in Europe, in Majorca and Normandy, in the eighteenth century. There the fabrics were called *chiné* prints — French for Chinese or Oriental — and were given softer, more delicate colors than those originating in the Middle East. Warp-printed fabrics became popular again with the "ethnic" designs prevalent in the late 1960s. In bold colors, these patterns worked well on contemporary furniture and had a trendy, Southwestern effect.

Classic Print Designs 🖋

Brunschwig & Fils's *Hampton Resist* is based on a pattern from another early printing technique (from a document in the Winterthur Museum). Resist patterns were made by applying wax to cloth and then immersing the cloth in dye. A second waxing and dipping produced varying shades of color.

Another Brunschwig & Fils print, *Sun, Moon, and Stars* — also from a document found in the Winterthur archives — was put into the

This advertisement featuring the Hampton Room in the Henry Francis du Pont Winterthur Museum in Delaware shows the original wax resist–dyed coverlet used to create *Hampton Resist*, a print on cotton and linen. The design has also been made into wallpaper.

This adaptation, *Sun, Moon, and Stars*, is from an early American documentary pattern found in the Henry Francis du Pont Winterthur Museum. It is seen here in Keith and Chippy Irvine's country house. The Chinese screen, painted floor, and Louis XVI chair provide a foil for the charmingly naive American design.

Opposite, inset: Michael Pick, of Stair & Co., was in charge of renovating the Art Moderne dining room and cocktail lounge of the Lansdowne Club, just off London's Berkeley Square. He used the very apt *Deco Rose* for the chair upholstery. Most of the house is in its original eighteenth-century style; it includes the Round Room, where the treaty of American Independence was drafted in 1783 when Lord Shelburne (later Lord Lansdowne) was prime minister. The private house was made into a club in 1935, and this lounge leading to the dining room recalls the 1930s ocean liner–style popular at the time of the club's inauguration.

collection years ago because of its delightful, naive quality. "The pattern was a real sleeper," according to Murray Douglas, "but designers and customers with style used it. The document was printed between 1790 and 1820 in sepia and madder (a brown and dark red combination on a beige ground), as was the reproduction. But only the 'new' colors sold. We have added the pattern to the wallpaper collection. We keep adding new colorings, which sell like crazy and have inspired many other sun, moon, and star patterns — and just think how old the original is."

Not all Brunschwig & Fils patterns are so classic. When *HG* wrote a story about chintz in July 1988, they photographed some

Brunschwig & Fils fabrics. They wanted to show some as-yet-unused documents from the Brunschwig archives. Not wanting to give away any prospective ideas, an Art Deco print that no one in the firm particularly liked was pulled out of the drawers — indeed, no one even wanted to take responsibility for its presence in the hallowed vaults! But when it appeared in the magazine, of course it turned out to be the one readers most desired. A couple of special orders were made, and as interest in Art Deco grew, the design was incorporated into the collection — mostly for "an eclectic audience," says Murray Douglas. "But it is important to do things like that so we are not known just for what's safe!"

This design appeared in an *HG* article as an example of what might be found in the Brunschwig archives. Readers then called, wanting it, and it was added to the Brunschwig collection, in four colorways on mohair twill, as *Deco Rose*.

This French design, called *Berry*, was a narrow, hand-blocked chintz when Ogden Codman used it at Codman House in Lincoln, Massachusetts, in the 1920s. When the house was restored Brunschwig reestablished the design, screen-printed on extra wide ground cloth.

Berry is a Brunschwig chintz named for the Berry region of central France. During the restoration of Ogden Codman's house in Lincoln, Massachusetts, it was discovered that Codman had slipcovered his chairs with *Berry* that he had bought in Paris in the 1920s. Replacement cloth was needed, because the original had faded. To illustrate how prices of prints can vary, the fabric was originally sold as a hand-blocked print thirty inches wide; but by the time of the Codman house restoration this narrow-width print had become too expensive for most customers. The Codman house restoration's special order prompted Brunschwig & Fils to see if it would be possible to screen-print the design on wider goods; as the Alsatian mill in France was able to print sixty-inch fabric, it was possible to offer double the width for less than a thirty-inch-wide hand-blocked print.

Verrières gives a cool, luxurious look to the Delft Room, a guest bedroom at the Inn at Depot Hill, Capitola-by-the-Sea, California (designed by Linda Floyd).

Today Brunschwig & Fils finds inspiration all over the world. A collection of timeless fabrics and wallpapers that would feel at home in either a traditional or a contemporary setting was created from documents found in the Benaki Museum. This museum, in Athens, Greece, displays objects from three thousand years of Hellenic culture, including Greek-influenced objects from the age of Sultan Süleyman the Magnificent. (See Chapter 10, p. 128, and Chapter 14, p. 162, for *Katia* matelassé, used by Charlotte Moss and Ralph Harvard, respectively; and Chapter 14, p. 160, for *Chrysso*, used by Lee Harris Pomeroy.)

One of Brunschwig & Fils's most popular designs is a three-color pattern consisting of a two-tone pattern on a ground color with a scalloped effect along the border. Inspired by an antique batik, the pattern

In Louise de Vilmorin's famous drawing room, every piece of furniture was upholstered in blue and white *Verrières*. The scalloped border was used in elegant, imaginative ways.

Verrières lends itself to many colorings. Here at Cawdor Castle, near Inverness, Scotland, Countess Cawdor selected a spirited pink version to dress the domed bed in one of the guest bedrooms. She chose Brunschwig's *Palampore* for another guest bedroom.

was designed by Jacques de Luze in Neuchâtel, Switzerland, and printed in 1810 in black, white, and red on a red-brown background. The pattern, now printed under license in the United States, comes from the venerable French fabric firm of Le Manach, where it is called *Batik*. It was used brilliantly by the stylish and influential poet, artist, and woman of the world Louise de Vilmorin in the drawing room of her family château, *Verrières*. The de Vilmorins were famous plantsmen and seedsmen, and the pattern has become known in America, where it is sold by Brunschwig, as *Verrières*, meaning "greenhouse."

With ideas gleaned from the traditional and the contemporary from every part of the globe, every spring and fall Brunschwig's representatives present fresh collections of textiles and other decorating products in showrooms around the world. Good design *is* forever, and Brunschwig & Fils proves it, finding inspiration from its archives, from museums, and from talented artists year after year, collection after collection.

Historical designs recur and live again and again, in subtly altered forms, to reflect their eras. Take, for example, the design known as *Beauport Promenade* (see Chapter 2, p. 48). This Indian elephant pattern was originally part of an elaborate wool shawl designed for the 1839 Paris Exposition. It reappeared, in a different guise, on a *mezzaro* — a type of shawl printed in Genoa in the early nineteenth century, usually with a tree of life form, worn by Genoese women. It was then adapted into a wallpaper design in the 1920s. Recently rediscovered, it is now used both for wallpaper and for fabric in the Brunschwig collection.

Such changes are natural progressions, revealing the spirit of each age. As Brunschwig & Fils moves into worldwide distribution, there will no doubt be many more changes to historical patterns, undreamed of as yet. The New York studio keeps a pulse on style shifts and anticipates customers' needs, sifting ideas from the collective consciousness of pacesetters in the arts, whether they are centered in the crucible of New York or wherever else fertile imaginations, energy, and creativity happen to be found.

Illustrating the versatility of the design, New York designer Tonin MacCallum decorated the bathroom of her own house in eastern Long Island with *Verrières* wallpaper. (See pp. 88–89 for a bedroom in blue *Verrières* by Mario Buatta.)

2

The Story of Brunschwig & Fils

This collection of family photographs includes Achille Brunschwig, in the center Art Nouveau frame (in front is a letter from him to his son, Roger, in the twenties, and next to it a copy of Colonel Brunschwig's book *La Légion d'Honneur*); Roger Brunschwig in his World War I uniform; a photograph of him later as Captain Brunschwig at his desk; in the small burl frame the four Comegys sisters as children; in a large frame at the back Mrs. B. wearing one of her "important" hats; next to it Mrs. B. and the young Murray Douglas together; and in the frame with the red mat, a color photograph of Brunschwig's president, Thomas Peardon, at his desk.

In 1857, a son named Achille was born into the Braunschweig family in Alsace, northeastern France. He was one of nine children.

The family's staunch allegiance to France caused them to leave Alsace when, together with Lorraine, it was annexed by Germany in 1871. As an industrial area with many textile mills, the border province had often changed hands, so the Braunschweig family records are difficult to trace and little is known about them. It is thought that the family went to Paris and Achille became involved with a textile business there. His son, Roger, was born in 1891. Records indicate that eight years later Achille co-owned one textile mill — or possibly two — called Brunschwig & Weil, north of Rheims, that produced tapestry fabrics.

Prior to World War I Achille also owned a mill in Aubusson, in central France, which according to a promotional brochure entitled *A Chat on Tapestry* manufactured tapestries and carpets. By this time Achille's business was known as Brunschwig & Fils. In keeping with the family's fondness for French culture, he had previously changed the family name to Brunschwig, which sounds less German.

Achille encountered many problems because of the territorial ambiguity of the Alsace-Lorraine region, which was savagely fought over during World War I, though both provinces were regained by France in the 1919 Treaty of Versailles. His mills went broke in 1934, for tapestry was no longer fashionable, but despite this he maintained superb connections with the textile industry. He stayed in the industry, opening an office in Paris to represent other textile mills instead of being a mill owner himself.

His dashing and handsome young son, Roger (the "fils"), showed little interest in textiles; he went into military service, becoming in 1916 the captain and commander of the 27th battalion of *Les Chasseurs*

Alpins. He led these elite and daring "Blue Devils" against German troops on the Vosges front, and was wounded seriously in the face. During the following months he underwent twenty-seven surgical operations. While hospitalized, he and several other soldiers with equally bad facial wounds decided to found the *Union des Blessés de la Face* (Union of the Face-Wounded but better and more slangily known as *Les Gueules Cassées*, "Broken Mugs" — men who became a familiar sight until the 1960s selling lottery tickets). The union was devoted to the treatment of those who were facially mutilated. At that time there was no special treatment or rehabilitation available for these men, though there was for soldiers who had suffered body wounds. Roger had facial reconstruction surgery and physical therapy for five years, and he believed such treatment should be available to others less fortunate. He got to know and appreciate many Americans who were in the forefront of the new skill of plastic surgery. His World War I awards included the Chevalier of the Légion d'Honneur, Officer of the Legion, and the Croix de Guerre.

The United States was a big and growing market that had never had access to the kind of textiles that Brunschwig & Fils carried. It was natural for Achille to suggest that his son go to America to tap in to its new prosperity. By 1925 Roger, then known as Captain Brunschwig, had opened an office at 383 Madison Avenue. He grew to love New York. He traveled by train across America, and at times met up with Paul Gadebusch — the partner of the decorative-fabric merchant Frederic Schumacher. According to Richard Slavin, the archivist and historian at Schumacher, Gadebusch noted in his diary that he had lunched and been to the races with Captain Brunschwig. There was a natural connection — the textile companies of Brunschwig, Schumacher, and Stroheim & Romann were all originally from Alsace. Captain Brunschwig visited Chicago, Texas, and California and made many friends — particularly in the West, because he was an excellent horseman. Everyone found him to be extremely charming. He proved to be a true salesman also, selling Brunschwig's imported fabrics to the then rather sparse number of decorators scattered throughout the country (in Seattle, for instance, there were but two at that time).

Possibly because of his wounds, Roger Brunschwig developed a special insight into people, and he was popular as a result. "My husband, Bradford, met and liked him during his West Coast days in California," said the late New Canaan decorator Jane Perin. "Bradford had an antiques and decorating shop out there then. He also told me no woman would ever marry Roger, because of his facial disfigurement."

But Bradford, it turned out, was wrong.

ZELINA

Zelina de Maclot Comegys — who was to become Captain Brunschwig's wife — had a French connection. Her mother's ancestors were originally Scottish Catholics called McLeod. To escape religious persecution when Scotland became Presbyterian, they left for France, owing to the Auld Alliance between the Catholics of Scotland and France (from the days of Mary, Queen of Scots). In France their name was translated to de Maclot. From France they immigrated first to Guadeloupe, then to New Orleans. Finally the de Maclots' descendants made their way up the Mississippi to St. Louis, in the early days of that city's history.

They must have become well established in that frontier town, for one of the de Maclot sons married the fourth daughter of the celebrated hostess Victoire Chouteau, a prominent woman known for bringing taste and culture to a then-unsophisticated St. Louis. A descendant of this union was Zelina de Maclot Comegys, born in Rock Island, Illinois.

Zelina was the eldest of four daughters (the others were Céleste, Amy, and Cornelia). None of the daughters learned French at an early age, and Zelina in particular was to regret it later. She would acquire a passion for French culture that would enrich and color her life and influence her work.

Their mother, Elise Virginia Comegys, died when the youngest, Cornelia (Connie), was 16. Though by then there was a growing number of women with taste and style in the region, their father, Dr. Joseph P. Comegys, decided the girls would be better educated in New York. Zelina had always wanted to be "in the arts," but at the time a career in the arts was not considered genteel for a girl. So she became a kindergarten teacher specializing in arts and crafts. In 1920 the family moved, and Zelina benefited from being in New York and studying at the Parsons School of Design.

Parsons was originally known as the New York School for Fine and Applied Arts and was later renamed after its founder, Frank Alvah Parsons. It was one of the few art schools that offered courses in the relatively new profession of interior decorating — and it offered them on quite a grand level. Frank Alvah Parsons stressed good housekeeping in particular. "All the students were in fear of him," says one of Mrs. Brunschwig's friends, decorator Ethel Smith, who graduated in 1926. "He was cruel to the less sophisticated kids from the

Zelina Comegys's watercolor sketches, such as this page from a notebook she kept while a student in Paris, were often of classical details that helped form her taste and influenced much of her later work.

Midwest. He'd ask, 'How is the butler going to get through that door?' " Mrs. Smith went on the very first trip taken by Parsons students to study for a year in Europe, a trip "which was totally disorganized. I took along my aunt as a chaperone, and so did some of the others."

William Odom, first a teacher and later the president of the school, was a strong influence on several generations of designers and decorators. He liked the richness and detail of eighteenth- and early-nineteenth-century French furniture, classical architecture, and luxurious, traditional fabrics. The school opened a branch in the Place des

This drawing from Zelina's sketchbook when she was at Parsons reveals a strong influence of Art Deco and the Bauhaus; but as can be seen in this scheme, a knowledge of traditional forms was very much part of the Parsons curriculum.

Vosges, which provided students a wonderful opportunity to look, learn, and sketch in Paris. The Parsons school in Paris gave Zelina Comegys her first serious look at the art of decoration. She graduated in 1929. That same year she gained a niece when a daughter, Murray, was born to her youngest sister, Connie Bartlett.

THE THIRTIES

After Parsons, Zelina got a job straightaway. She was employed as a designer by McMillen, an interior decorating firm that only took on Parsons graduates. Zelina knew the founder of the firm, Eleanor McMillen (later Mrs. Brown), who was born in St. Louis and had attended Parsons. The world of *le haut décor* was small then: William Odom bought antiques in Europe for Eleanor McMillen; Zelina became a close friend of Ethel Smith, another much-respected designer, who worked at McMillen until she retired in the 1980s; and Zelina herself was known to babysit for Eleanor McMillen's son.

Most of the decorators from that era talk about the fun they had then, despite the Depression. They were their drinking years, all the more potent because of Prohibition. There were parties with bathtub gin: "My parents had a pet alligator they kept in the bath that had to be

Zelina Brunschwig in her office with a photograph of her husband and Humphrey Bogart.

moved to make room for the bathtub gin," says Murray Douglas. Ethel Smith remembers the time they bought applejack from a Millbrook farmer in the countryside north of New York City. A truckload of it arrived at the McMillen offices, and the bookkeeper — a Christian Scientist — was furious at having to sign for it.

According to Betty Sherrill, now President of McMillen, it was at McMillen that Zelina learned to "scheme" a room using swatches. She was going to find this skill especially useful in the years ahead.

Jane Perin, another McMillenite, said, "Zelina didn't like me too much at first, though we ended up good friends. I had just got married and was blissfully ecstatic, you see, but she was never really happy until she met Roger."

On a working trip to Paris, Zelina had to expedite a special order of beige brocatelle that seemed to have become snarled up. Never one to give up, she kept badgering the Brunschwig & Fils office on the tiny Rue des Petits-Champs. Captain Brunschwig was not enthusiastic about dealing with this persistent American woman, but his secretary, Mlle. Goumaz, said: "*Capitain*, you had better invite this lady for lunch, as she is very upset." She knew that, with his wonderful Gallic manners, Captain Brunschwig would pacify her.

It was a successful lunch. Zelina, described once by Elizabeth MacRae Boykin of the *Washington Post* as "very smart, with blue eyes, as American as apple pie and a Colonial Dame," was 40. He was 45. Neither had ever married. They found they had much in common, particularly their passion for quality and their fascination with interesting people.

When Zelina got back to the United States she confided to Ethel Smith how much she liked Captain Brunschwig. It was mutual, for soon he came to visit her in New York. As Mrs. Smith said, "It was obvious they were very much in love." Just as everything was going swimmingly, Captain Brunschwig suddenly returned to Paris. Zelina cried on Ethel's shoulder. She felt she had lost him — he hadn't mentioned marriage!

Mrs. Smith was in her apartment a week later when she was astounded to find, ringing her doorbell, both Zelina and Roger, radiating happiness. Zelina simply displayed her hand; on it was an engagement ring. Evidently Roger had been on the brink of marrying someone else, a Parisian woman who was married, with children, but about to get a divorce. He'd had to go back and explain his sudden *coup de foudre* and ask to be released.

Captain Brunschwig and Zelina were married on July 25, 1938. Mrs. Smith remembers the date vividly because she was giving birth to her son Rob and couldn't attend the wedding. The next morning visitors made a commotion outside her hospital room. The nurse insisted, "You can't go into the room!" but in strode the Captain and Mrs. B., with masses of flowers left over from their wedding.

The marriage was remarkably successful. Their talents and strengths were different, but their similar interests outweighed their differences. The Captain (later the Colonel) was a businessman whose word and handshake were his bond. He was respected for his sense of honor and he was liked for his charm. Zelina was volatile, creative, more abrasive than Roger, energetic, and a perfectionist, and therefore she was relentless. Together they made a perfect team. Achille meantime stepped out of the picture, retiring to the sunshine of Nice, and the *fils* became president of the company.

The World War II Years

During the war, Brunschwig's European sources dried up with the occupation of France. An office was maintained in Paris, but it could not ship anything. All they had in America was the stock on the shelves. Roger Brunschwig, realizing that the war effort was far more important than his business, joined General de Gaulle in England in 1941 and later served with the Free French in North Africa, France, and Germany.

Zelina Brunschwig quit McMillen and took her husband's place in his business. Mrs. B. realized that the company, cut off from Europe, would have to become independent and more American. There was no silk and very little wool, so she experimented with other fibers, such as rayon (but in those days it was unwashable and its dyes undependable). One novel fabric, for instance, called Bomber cloth, was made of synthetic fiber woven to be very strong. Fabrics became democratic and luxury unfashionable. Because cotton was one of the few fibers available, Brunschwig's textiles took on a lighter appearance that was immediately more informal in feeling and echoed the clearer, sunnier light of the whole North American continent. The transformation was stimulating. Colors that had been seen in clothing but never in decorating set a tone that was thoroughly modern yet retained traditional roots.

In spite of the changed, less formal way of life, at no time did Brunschwig & Fils alter its strict rules about selling only to the trade.

This policy helped make possible the growth of the decorating and design profession in America, a business no other country shares to quite the same degree. To this day Brunschwig sells only to the trade, and will let into their showrooms retail customers only if they are accompanied by their decorator, designer, or architect or if they have a dated letter with their designer's signature.

Influencing decoration at this time were a number of strong-minded women who became both taste makers and businesspeople: Nancy McClelland, who collected and reproduced documentary wall-papers; Alice Beer at the downtown Cooper-Hewitt Museum; textile experts like Cora Ginsburg and Elinor Merrell; Edith Standen of the Museum of Modern Art, who specialized in tapestries; and Mary Allis, a decorator and antique dealer, who was involved in preservation and restoration. Still influenced by the Colonial Revival movement, their prevailing taste was for English and sometimes eighteenth-century French furnishings.

Mrs. B. handled the business on her own and proved more than competent. She made several canny marketing moves. One was to use her decorating experience, which gave her the idea of "scheming," a novel concept at the time. She saw to it that every showroom sample carried swatches of complementary fabrics that could be used to deco-rate a room, creating multiple sales. Very few textile salespeople had decorating experience, so she was way ahead. She also made the clever and quite bold move of hiring the now-legendary but then-pioneering public relations expert Eleanor Lambert, who dreamed up events such as the Designers Show, a student design competition co-sponsored by the Metropolitan Museum of Art. Brunschwig & Fils reproduced the top three designs and incorporated them into their collections. Mrs. B. believed that modern artists should be given a chance: "In the eigh-teenth century," she said, "it was the designers and artists of the day who were popular and who produced the designs still considered best of all by many Americans. But we can't stick only to traditional things. We must develop ideas for ourselves, by ourselves, designs that are typical of today and as right for today as those eighteenth-century designs were for that day."

The prevalence of cotton led Mrs. B. to a firm belief in the use of slipcovers. "They avoid that very tight rigid look," she said, "and they can be removed easily for cleaning and changed with the seasons if desired." Her views and opinions on decoration and textiles were frequently quoted in the trade papers and decorating magazines.

Taking advantage of Brunschwig's scheming, a customer in the New York showroom makes a note of possible fabrics and trimmings to use with *Cavendish* glazed chintz.

When Roger, by now Colonel Brunschwig, returned in 1946 he could not believe his eyes. He was thrilled to find the American office organized and doing well. Mrs. B. was inspired not only by established European designs but was now also looking to such things as modern painting, fashion, and ballet for ideas. Indeed, Brunschwig's present distinctive style was established during those years — a fusion of traditional French taste with relaxed, practical American flair. The Brunschwig & Fils aesthetic represented a jolt of energy to the world of decorative textiles in the second half of the twentieth century that paralleled the vigor of European textiles in the eighteenth century brought about by the introduction of painted *indiennes* and *toiles de Jouy*.

The Second Half of the Twentieth Century

Achille, who in Paris had always been a dapper *boulevardier*, enjoyed Nice to the utmost. He went to a tea dance every afternoon — including the day he died, in 1949 — at the Hôtel des Cigognes, where he lived out the last years of his life.

Colonel Brunschwig had retaken charge of the business side of the firm, while Zelina ran the design side. Colonel Brunschwig also became very involved with what was known as the French colony in New York. Mrs. B. was well dressed, impeccably groomed, and a perfect hostess both for the business and the French colony. For her efforts on behalf of the Free French war relief and for her contributions to French design, she was given the Chevalier of the Légion d'Honneur by the French government in 1951. In addition to his many accolades, in 1965 the Colonel was awarded the highest honor of all, the Grand Croix of the Légion d'Honneur, by his own general, de Gaulle, in person.

One of the consequences of the post–World War II era was the revival of France's luxury fabric business. As the textile industry began to reawaken, many French mill owners looked at the American market for distribution and to the son of their friend Achille. Colonel Brunschwig was familiar with all the sons of his father's colleagues and suggested to them a way to show a whole new audience of Americans the glories of French design. The Colonel's idea was to buy minimal yardage to make rack and memo samples for every Brunschwig & Fils showroom, and to set up a telex system for designers to order cut yardage through Brunschwig's Paris office, which became a buying office. No inventory was needed, and the orders were flown to America via the rapidly growing air freight network. Delivery of these superior and glamorous fabrics usually took three weeks. Advertisements in trade and decorating magazines featured "fabrics from France" with photographs of the Paris skyline, the Seine and the Eiffel Tower in the foreground.

In the 1950s, before the Decoration and Design Building on Third Avenue in New York was established, prestigious decorative textile showrooms were scattered in the midtown area. There was, however, a definite route that designers took to shop for fabrics. To quote Chippy Irvine's husband, decorator Keith Irvine: "The first stop was Brunschwig & Fils. I was so impressed with how fabulous the Brunschwig showrooms looked when I first arrived from England — all the luxe of France but with fresh, clear American colors. Very Billy Baldwin. Then you hit Margowen — the name derived from owner Margaret Owen, now gone — which had delightful Susanne Fontan–designed prints; then Rose Cumming; next was Kent Bragaline; then Fortuny — who then seemed impossible to deal with; then the Tillets. It was also the time of Nordic moderns like Jack Lenor Larsen and Marimekko. Then, in the early 1960s, I named and cofounded Clarence House, though I am no longer a part of it." Now most of the more sophisticated decorative fabric companies have showrooms in the Decoration and Design Building.

In 1945 Mrs. B. took on her sister Connie, a graduate of Columbia University's Teachers College, as showroom manager, a post Connie held until 1965. "Connie Bartlett was always friendly and helpful," remembers New York designer and Parsons graduate Hector Grant. "She was a great problem solver," Keith Irvine recalls. "If anything went wrong, we'd always say, 'Get Mrs. Bartlett,' and she'd manage to put it right."

In 1955 Mrs. B.'s niece, Murray, joined the firm and worked in the design studio, becoming director of the studio in the 1960s. Wallpapers were added to the Brunschwig product line on her watch, and by 1964 wallpapers and borders were a regular part of the collection and another arm of the company.

As the 1960s dawned, Mrs. B. realized that Americans lacked a basic knowledge of French textiles, especially French terms. So in 1964 she organized a traveling exhibition, with an accompanying illustrated booklet, called *The Tradition of French Fabrics*. Murray called on a New York designer and display specialist with vast historical knowledge, Donald MacMillen, to put the show together. Advertising consultant Ben Givaudan acted as an adviser, and Murray Douglas was the

Detail of display for the 1962 traveling exhibition of "The Tradition of French Fabrics" by Brunschwig & Fils.

in-house liaison. The exhibit gave historical background on the evolution of traditional French styles, with actual examples of fabrics and a few precious documents. The show made its debut at the Albany Institute of History and Art and traveled to the Taft Museum in Cincinnati. Then the Smithsonian Institution's traveling exhibition program sent it around the United States. The exhibition solidified Brunschwig's French connection and gave it credibility with museums and historical societies, which was particularly important as the surge of interest in preservation mushroomed with the approach of the Bicentennial.

One of the fringe benefits of Brunschwig's association with Donald MacMillen was access to his circle of antique dealers, curators, and museum contacts. "Through him we met John A. H. Sweeney, Henry Francis du Pont's assistant, and director Charles Montgomery and his wife, Florence, head of Winterthur's textile study room," recalls Murray Douglas. "We were asked to develop reproductions of early American textile designs for a new exhibition area at Winterthur." Though Brunschwig received no public credit for this work, it gained the confidence of Winterthur's management; and when Winterthur was ready to put reproduction fabric in their displays, they turned to Brunschwig. Ross Francis, Brunschwig's vice president of development, has kept up the relationship to this day.

Mrs. B.'s private wish was to develop a collection of historic textiles that would be used not only for restoration work but also for present-day interiors. She had seen the power of Schumacher's connection with Williamsburg and knew a collaboration with Winterthur would be rewarding. Beginning slowly, with patterns like *Hampton Resist* (Chapter 1, p. 21), *China Fancy*, and *Sultan of Gujarat* (Chapter 10, p. 131), the Brunschwig-Winterthur collection now includes wallpapers, resists, needlework, and a Norwich stripe — a cloth with figured wool stripes and an ombré effect in the warp — all developed from the museum's vast holdings.

Trimmings (passementerie) were added at Brunschwig in 1967. The selection ranged from simple braids to elaborately decorated, fringed or tasseled extravaganzas made by hand in France. The collection opened with ninety-five designs, including some 330 trimming colors stocked in New York on braids, gimps, tapes, fringes, tiebacks, and borders — and it has since grown larger.

Always looking for a good business opportunity, Brunschwig in the 1960s began designing products for contract work, manufacturing fabrics and wallpapers in large quantities for use in the offices and public buildings that were mushrooming at the time. A special contract division was set up to handle the increased volume of production. This division worked with designers who specialized in large office buildings, apartment houses, hotels, restaurants, banks, and other commercial areas, serving customers that wanted the Brunschwig look without quite as many colors as were found in prints from the regular collection. The division added many textured wovens, and it offered a touch of traditional elegance and distinction to the stereotypical interiors found in so many of the new buildings. For those younger couples just starting out and for more casual second homes, a line of carefully designed but less expensive cottons was created, named the Maisonnette collection.

Just as Murray Douglas became involved with the design studio, following her aunt's footsteps both figuratively and physically, her cousin Tom Peardon, Céleste's son, was echoing the Colonel's work on the business side. The Brunschwigs had no children of their own, and they became very close to their American nephew and niece. They were, however, hard taskmasters, with Mrs. B. being especially demanding of everyone, herself included. Both Tom Peardon and Murray Douglas started at the bottom and had to work their way up.

When Colonel Roger E. Brunschwig died on December 7th, 1972, at age 81, Tom Peardon became Brunschwig's president in his place. The Colonel was the most highly decorated French officer residing in the United States at the time of his unexpected death at New York Hospital. He was buried in France with full military honors.

Gradually Mrs. B. began to give up the reins, though never entirely. Almost to the last she would appear in the showroom, using a cane, feisty as ever. Designer Gary Crain remembers one time when a woman in the Brunschwig showroom was challenged when it was discovered that she had no account there. Mrs. B., overhearing the conversation, brandished her cane and shouted, "You do *not* have an account here! Get out, get out!"

In 1980, the year before she died, Mrs. B. saw to it that Brunschwig & Fils celebrated its one hundredth anniversary. It seems in retrospect to have been an arbitrary milestone, decided solely by Mrs. B., for no real historic evidence can be found to substantiate 1880 as the founding date of the company. But who could argue? True to her indomitable nature, and possibly because she realized she did not have much time left (and it was, after all, a nice round number), *that's* when she wanted the centennial, so that's when she got it!

Fabric, wallpaper, trimmings, and furniture are transported across America in this truck with the familiar *Brunschwig* check and red logo on its side. Here it is seen with the Manhattan skyline in the distance.

The Present Generation 🖎

THE NORTH WHITE PLAINS PLANT

In the past fifteen years, under the present generation of the family, Brunschwig & Fils has made major expansions. Part of this growth took place as a result of the company's 1982 decision to move its corporate headquarters and warehouse to North White Plains, north of New York City. Dwarfing the Manhattan offices and nestled in a pleasantly landscaped and well-maintained ten-acre expanse, the Brunschwig building was adapted from a Chevrolet dealership that comprised a rotunda showroom attached to a huge garage. Despite its size and functional, officelike demeanor, there is a courteous and much-encouraged family feeling about the place.

The lobby of the main entrance is hung with large photographs of present-day craftsmen working eighteenth-century French hand looms. Executive offices circle the rotunda on the floor above the lobby, installed when the building was adapted. Beyond the rotunda are further offices, some individual, others divided into open-topped enclosures. As in the New York offices, attention is paid to visual details. On a wall in one corridor hangs a framed antique map of Paris; on another is a photograph of Brunschwig & Fils's huge delivery truck, in the gray-and-white-check and red lettering that makes up the company's distinctive logo, with Manhattan's skyscrapers in the distance.

One area of the offices is given over to people taking orders over the telephone. "We have customers who think that talking directly to

Overleaf: Six aisles the length of a football field hold Brunschwig & Fils products on tall shelves in the North White Plains warehouse.

the North White Plains office instead of their local showroom will save time," says Mr. Peardon. "In reality it all goes on the same computer system, but the personal touch can be important." The all-important computer room is manned day and night. London, which has its own Brunschwig & Fils showroom, kicks in at four A.M., Paris at three; meanwhile the West Coast drops out, then New York. Sales offices exist even in Tokyo and China. Rather like the East India Company in its prime, Brunschwig & Fils is a global enterprise upon which the sun never sets.

One large area is entirely devoted to making samples and cuttings. Stitchers sit at machines, overlocking the edges of memo samples. Some of the samples are huge, because they must show a repeat that is large enough for a designer to drape over a chair or hold up to simulate drapery so a client can make a decision. Small cuttings used for color reference are pinked around the edges and labeled. Very expensive textile samples — such as handwoven French brocaded silks — are pierced, slightly off-center, with large metal eyelets so the unscrupulous won't be tempted to squirrel them off for cushions. Thousands of samples and swatches are stacked in piles on shelves, for the sample room supplies and replenishes Brunschwig & Fils showrooms all across the world. This is a very necessary part of the business, but it is also costly; customers occasionally retain more than five hundred dollars' worth of samples to bring in not much more than that in sales.

The arrival of a consolidated shipment at the loading dock is a frequent but always exciting event. Bolts of fabric from France, England, Switzerland, Italy, and America come in. France is still the number one foreign supplier, but now American fabrics make up about 35 percent of the total. In order to maintain quality, every piece is put onto a roller machine and examined before being relegated to its shelf. Rafael Guerrero, the warehouse manager, runs the ground-floor stock-room, the most impressive part of the whole complex. Aisles the length of a football field are packed floor to ceiling with rolls of fabrics, wall-papers, and trimmings, each with its own bar code — requiring some twenty thousand sales-keeping units (SKUs) in all. The high top shelves can only be reached by mechanized high-low trollies that operate like cherry pickers, and if you happen to wander in the aisles with them bearing down on either side they seem as menacing as some automated creatures out of an H. G. Wells novel.

In the shipping area a processing system tracks 95 percent of the goods that are shipped. The largest number of customers at the present time are in the New York area, with Atlanta second and Los Angeles third largest.

Brunschwig & Fils remains to this day a family business with strong ties to its French roots. The Franco-American tradition has reached its third generation with Tom Peardon, Jr., who was named president in 1973. Mr. Peardon, an American with a French-born wife, is the grand-nephew by marriage of the company's founder, Achille Brunschwig. Colonel Brunschwig's sister had two sons in France, Jean and André Chognard. They shared his inheritance but they are no longer involved with the business.

Mr. Peardon graduated from Harvard College in 1960 with a degree in geology. His career has taken him, he says, "from rocks to rags," though he had no such plans when he graduated. "I didn't intend to join the family business, but my aunt and uncle suggested I work here 'temporarily' until I had to join the military." His job turned out to be a lifetime career. Tom Peardon married Eveline Le Jemtel in 1968. They have one son, Olivier. The Peardons live in a restored 1785 house in Connecticut. His interest in eighteenth- and nineteenth-century architecture has led to Mr. Peardon's serving on the board of trustees of the Antiquarian and Landmarks Society in Hartford, Connecticut, as well as his being a strong supporter of Brunschwig's traditional collections. "I'm a firm believer in the American public's interest in interior design. They've been concerned with the décor of the home for some time, but now that has spread to commercial spaces as well. While we never intend to abandon residential work, we've become more involved in the contract, hospitality, and health care areas, and have initiated a furniture collection. Our clients have been trying to buy the chairs off the showroom floor for years, and now we are finally thrilled to let them."

Like the Colonel, Mr. Peardon concentrates on the business side, while his cousin, Murray Douglas — like Mrs. B. — is involved with the aesthetic direction of the company. She is now the senior vice president in charge of public relations and advertising, and the company spokesperson.

THE DESIGN TEAM

Murray's Aunt Zelina was a strong influence on her as a child. She regaled her niece with tales of French chivalry and knights in walled towns like Carcassonne. Often she would work in bed in her smart apartment, wearing wonderfully luxurious silk bed jackets and insisting

Murray Douglas, senior vice president and co-owner of Brunschwig & Fils, sits on a chair of *Leopard* velvet in her attractive office overlooking Manhattan.

that Murray feel the fabulous fabric, making her aware of style and discriminating taste.

The first time Murray met her new uncle, Captain Brunschwig, she and her Girl Scout chums were warned about his facial wounds, which, she was told, gave him a strange appearance. But she and her friends were charmed and impressed, and he became a kind of hero to them. One time he asked Murray if she'd ever heard of Charles Boyer. Had she ever! He actually *knew* her favorite movie star? Captain Brunschwig gave her a photo signed "To Murray from Charles Boyer, with love and kisses," and she just swooned!

As she grew up, Murray wanted to be a painter. She majored in art at Skidmore College. During the summer she worked with her aunt at Brunschwig, when the showroom was at 509 Madison Avenue. Her third year she spent in France with Skidmore's junior year program. Her uncle arranged for her to stay with a French family. "I suspect it may have been with the woman my uncle almost married," says Murray, "for when Mrs. B. found out she wasn't too pleased — in fact she was very jealous!"

The Skidmore program included the famous Cours de Civilisation at the Sorbonne and intensive art history at the Ecole du Louvre. She studied with Fernand Léger, who was one of the few working artists who had an atelier in Paris in 1949. Murray worked alongside Americans studying in Paris on the G.I. Bill. "Léger didn't like young women much," Murray remembers. "He told me I had an artistic future, but not as a painter." Devastated, she returned to the States, got her degree from Skidmore, and had no idea what direction to take. Mrs. B. suggested she try Parsons's summer school interior design course — and generously offered to pay for it. "I took to it like a duck to water and felt rather superior for having lived in Europe," says Murray. She adds, however, that she really was unaware of the advantages she'd had until two students on the G.I. Bill said wistfully how lucky she was to have been around fine interior design so much of her life.

It was a good time to be studying at Parsons. Albert Hadley — of Parish-Hadley — was teaching there full-time, as was the famous Stanley Barrows. Billy Baldwin was a Parsons critic.

After graduating from Parsons in 1953, Murray married and went with her American husband to live in Linz, Austria. The following year they had a son, Russel. After a couple more years, Mrs. B. thought it high time her niece returned to America; she offered her a job as an apprentice in the Brunschwig studio in 1955.

Like her Aunt Zelina, Murray Douglas sketched in her notebooks when she went to Paris with her class from Parsons. Here is a page of decorative objects in the Musée des Arts Décoratifs.

Having previously studied painting at the Léger atelier in Paris, Murray Douglas showed proficiency in her watercolor sketches by the time she came to Europe with her class from Parsons. "I learned so much from our trip to Europe with Parsons," says Murray Douglas, "and sketching really helps to commit details to your memory."

After a year in the studio, Murray became decorator Polly Jessup's assistant in Palm Beach, Florida, where she gained practical, hands-on knowledge, such as how curtains are made, how wallpaper is restored, and how to match colors of paint. With this training she returned to the studio, where she eventually became design director. She expanded the fabric collections, extended the company's collaboration with museums, and developed the wallpaper collections.

Since 1990, though she's still a voice in the design area, Mrs. Douglas has been the head of advertising and public relations. ("The best job in the firm," quips her cousin Tom.) Murray is now married to the writer and investment adviser Albert Douglas.

Ross Johnson Francis, Brunschwig's vice president of development, joined the company in 1968. A southerner — with a distinct accent to prove it — Ross was born in Winston-Salem, North Carolina. In the Brunschwig tradition, she too studied interior design at Parsons. In her class was interior decorator William Hodgins, who later designed Brunschwig's first Boston showroom in his refined, pared-down classical style. Ross Francis is responsible for setting the themes of the Brunschwig fabric and wallpaper collections and making them a reality. Reflecting Brunschwig style, with its reverence for good design, is part of her job. Together with Paul Dobrowolski, Ross guides each new and ongoing collection — choosing print and woven fabrics, traveling abroad to find new mills and design sources, selecting wallpaper patterns, expanding and refining the already broad scope of Brunschwig ideas for residential and contract markets.

Paul Dobrowolski has been the design director of the studio in New York since 1990. He is in charge of the artists who create fabric and wallpaper designs.

For many years, one of Brunschwig & Fils's greatest assets has been its archival trove of fabric and wallpaper documents. Since 1983, when archivist and curator Judith Straeten joined the company, the archives have been more efficiently researched, cataloged, mounted, photographed, and stored than ever before.

Judy was born in La Jolla, California, and grew up in Staten Island, New York, Japan, and Baltimore. She was an assistant curator of costume at the Metropolitan Museum of Art from 1971 until 1980, and she was directly involved with eight of the now legendary exhibitions associated with fashion maven Diana Vreeland. She has many tales to tell about those days. A lecturer, conservator, editor, writer, and curator, Judy Straeten has championed the rewards and pleasures

The fabric *Beauport Promenade* was made after a wallpaper found at SPNEA-owned Beauport House in Gloucester, Massachusetts.

of historical research on wallpaper and fabrics — both with respect to decoration as well as to fashion.

Patrick Mongiello, Brunschwig's vice president of marketing and sales, oversees eighteen Brunschwig & Fils American showrooms and fifteen foreign sales representatives throughout the world, with the help of Robert Raymond, director of export sales. The director of operations, who takes care of everything not covered by Patrick Mongiello's sales and marketing position, is Nancy Weir. Nancy started in the firm as Mrs. B.'s secretary, a job she found to be excellent training for her current wide-ranging responsibilities.

North Carolinian Lewis Paul is in charge of product development, namely, hard-frame furniture and special collections, including lamps and tables. Thomas Marshall, special products manager, is responsible for overseeing the development of all special or custom-ordered fabric, wallpaper, trim, and furniture made by Brunschwig & Fils. Tom's job often requires working with a museum house — such as the Webb-Deane-Stevens Museum in Connecticut or Gunston Hall in Virginia — to reproduce a documentary wallpaper or have a special fabric made. "If there is an actual document in existence, it is better to work directly from it," Tom maintains. "If this is impossible — museums are loathe to let these precious items leave the premises — accurately made, true-scale photographs are used." Brunschwig has a number of commissioned or freelance artists on tap who can go to these museums to make watercolor patches to ensure the tones are accurate. When asked for special fabrics to use in period rooms where there is no original, Tom consults with Judy Straeten in the Brunschwig archives to find historically correct ideas to suggest to the customer.

The minimum length required for specially printed fabric is fifty yards. Small amounts like this can be expensive, because special screens have to be designed and made; the more cloth a customer orders, the less expensive each yard is. For wallpaper, fifteen rolls is the minimum order. For custom work, Brunschwig can call upon eight different wallpaper mills, three fabric-printing plants, and six mills that do custom weaving. Some special orders are for different colorways of existing Brunschwig fabrics. Not all commissions are documentary reproductions, nor, indeed, traditional. "Sometimes they are plain weird!" says Tom Marshall. "We get odd requests, like the one for custom-dyed leather in fuchsia and turquoise, embossed with a faux ostrich pattern. But we did it — for twenty-five dollars a square foot!" He sends a sample of every special order to the New York studio, in case the

High above Manhattan, the studio at Brunschwig & Fils enjoys a superb northern light that is the envy of most European studios. Here Vice President of Development Ross Francis and Design Director Paul Dobrowolski work with Brunschwig's skilled artists.

design team eventually wants to incorporate the idea into a collection. "I never try to influence the regular collections, because what I work on has little to do with style trends. We do things that are a law unto themselves." Tom is also responsible for the actual production of all custom-made items, including furniture. He collaborates closely with Lewis Paul in the production of articles such as lamps and tables. Brunschwig considers its custom services, which are often unavailable elsewhere, an integral part of its business.

It would be impossible to name every person who reinforces the running of an enterprise as large as Brunschwig & Fils. Every showroom has a sales manager and a team of salespeople. But despite its size, Brunschwig tries to greet every customer in a personal way. None of those named here could perform their duties without the hard work and devotion of the many artists, colorists, design schemers, salespeople, secretaries, swatchmakers, packers, maintenance people — and even the baseball team! — who are part of Brunschwig & Fils.

3 🌿

Trimmings

Professional interior designers have long known that trimmings serve an important visual purpose in a room, embellishing fabric, offering counterpoint, or adding just the right authoritative touch. In the latter part of the 1960s, when the general public began to show a serious interest in decoration, there was a growing sense that rooms looked unfinished without the subtle addition of trimmings made of something other than the predominant fabric. Brunschwig & Fils presented its first trimmings collection in 1967, to serve its customers better and to enhance the company's fabric collections.

Trimmings — fringes, tassels, cording, tapes, and braids — have been used on clothing, harnesses, tents, and awnings since earliest times, in ancient Egypt, Assyria, Persia, China, India, and all the countries around the Mediterranean.

By the thirteenth century the French had applied these decorations to the interiors of their houses. Those who made trimmings joined the proud ranks of other French craftsmen by joining trade unions organized to regulate apprenticeships and the relations between patrons and craftsmen; rules were imposed to ensure the honesty of artisans and merchants. The French term for "trimming" is *la passementerie;* this became the name used officially for all the various Parisian trimming trades in 1564.

The French take their trade skills seriously. They write histories and hold exhibitions, including shows featuring the many variations of passementerie. Trying to decipher the French terms used in connection with passementerie is as good as an advanced French lesson, for it is a craft with a specialized vocabulary. Some of the terms are quite poetic, describing often complex workmanship: *giselles* are supple silk fringes with a lacy quality (often called fan-edge fringes in America); *jasmins* are chains of tiny silk-covered loops and flowerlike motifs; *noisettes* are

The most elaborate and sophisticated passementeries are made in Paris. These tasseled tiebacks were shown at the Bagatelle show of Braquenié fabrics; they can be special-ordered in America through Brunschwig & Fils.

Fred Cannon of David Anthony Easton, Inc. trimmed the *Janvry* coral damask covering the sofa in his Brooklyn house with *Lilibet* small rope and *Clémentine* small fringe, both made in France.

Racks in the Brunschwig & Fils New York showroom display a variety of tasseled tiebacks.

small nut shapes covered in silk threads; and *macarons* are flat buttonlike motifs named after the almond-flavored Italian cookie. Both *jasmins* and *macarons* are often formed from little bands of parchment, vellum, cardboard *(cartisane)*, or wire, covered in silky threads.

When Brunschwig decided to offer trimmings among their wares, it was to France, the most sophisticated source of passementerie, that they turned. Though some Brunschwig trimmings are manufactured in Italy, England, or the United States, France is still their biggest supplier. Many French passementerie terms have crept into Brunschwig & Fils product names, including *Frange* (fringe) and *Nid d'Abeille* (Honeycomb).

Many French products today are composed of viscose and spun rayon as well as beautiful but somewhat more perishable silk.

Since the first Brunschwig trimmings collection was introduced, the number of items and colorways has grown. Showrooms now display waterfalls of glistening tiebacks — wonderful twisted cords culminating in glorious outsize tassels dripping with diminutive tassels or strings of *jasmins*. Each tassel is based on a wooden form or *moule*, which usually has a head, body, and foot (*tête, corps*, and *pied*). These *moules* come in different shapes — pear, onion, olive, radish, drum, sugarloaf, and so on. The names of these shapes echo the everyday objects of pre-revolutionary French village life where these silken passementerie were first manufactured. The "skirt" *(jupe)* of the tassel, if it has one, hangs from a throat *(gorge)* or a waist *(ceinture)*. The head and body can be embellished in many different ways, such as with spirals, netting, crisscrosses, or chevrons. The throat or waist might be studded with *pois* (flat button-shaped decorations), *guirlande* (garlands formed from *cartisane* or guipure), or *macarons*. To this day most elabo-

Edging a delicate curtain in a room designed by Clare Fraser is *Fujita* fringe, made of transparent beads.

rate tassels are handmade by craftspeople working *à l'établi* — at a work table — rather than at a loom or machine.

Trimming cords (or ropes, if they are thick) are made of plied yarns twisted together in many different ways. Sometimes it takes two strong men to twist a heavy rope to the right tension. Knowing how labor-intensive they are to make, it is easy to see how sometimes a tieback, or *embrasse,* as the French say, can cost as much as the curtain fabric itself.

Cords are sometimes used instead of fabric-covered welts to trim cushions or upholstery. To avoid having to hand-sew the cord around the cushion, a flange of tape is attached to the cord, which can then be trapped into the seam.

Fringes are made of everything from heavy bullion to wood molds, crystal beads, *bouclés* (loops), and marabout (which imitates the look of feather boas). There are knotted fringes, tasseled fringes, block fringes (usually straight-cut fringe in blocks of color, though they can also have a more delicate fan edge), and fluffy moss fringes. Machines have been invented over the centuries to perform certain tasks in the manufacture of trims, but handwork is still essential for complex parts of the job.

Gimp is a narrow flat braid with a three-dimensional quality; it is used to cover the heads of upholstery tacks, to trim lampshades, and to embellish luxurious cushions. *Crêtes,* from the French word for crests, are wider and are made of large and small silk-covered loops, often set on either side of a stable band. Tape is usually both softer and simpler than gimp or *crêtes.* Borders are wider than gimp or tape and are usually woven on specialized looms, though again, handwork may be needed for certain fancy varieties. In Brunschwig showrooms, gimps, borders, fringes, and tapes are shown in sets on display boards and included in fabric display "schemes."

As with an elegant wallpaper border, or a fine French mat around a watercolor, or an engaging welt or gimp "frame" around a needle-point cushion, the effect of the right passementerie can't be over-stressed. These details give the finishing touch, containing or "fencing" a textile in a professional way. Decorators have access to wonderful embellishments that nonprofessionals seldom see. Whether a modest tape or a grand bullion fringe, the right trimming serves to amplify the use of a chosen fabric and give a masterful quality to a room. However, as Mrs. Douglas often warns, resist the temptation to overuse *la passe-menterie.* There is no need to gild the lily.

4 Wallpaper

At a propitious moment in 1959, Brunschwig & Fils began to think about adding wallpaper to its product line. Mrs. B. and Murray Douglas knew wallpaper could transform a room optically — by making it appear taller with up-reaching vertical patterns, or by pushing the walls out with scenic effects, or by bringing the outdoors inside with garden greenery and architectural details. A wall covering can create the illusion of a more spacious room than there actually is. A good example is the Pompeian room at the Met. The room is long and narrow with a vaulted ceiling, but the wall painting makes it look so open you forget you're in a tight rectangle.

One day Ted Griffith, Brunschwig's San Francisco representative, came triumphantly into the New York studio with wallpaper samples in hand based on Brunschwig fabric designs! He too had thought about adding a wallpaper collection, and he had gone ahead and had samples made of several existing designs. The best sample was of *Bengali*, a one-color toile pattern that is still going strong both as wallpaper and fabric. Brunschwig soon found printers in the East and picked out more already-existing designs for the first collection, including Ted's other designs. These met with such enthusiasm from clients that Brunschwig delved back into the archives to find more patterns.

By 1964, wallpapers and borders were a regular part of the collection and another arm of the company. Louis Bowen, a friend of Mrs. B. who had a fine wallpaper business and was a great observer of the decorating scene, proved especially helpful. The wallpaper collections included patterns on vinyl and papers that could be treated with protective finishes for easy maintenance.

Brunschwig's design team followed Nancy McClelland's lead. She was one of the first American women to take a serious interest in and write about documentary wallpapers. She had reproduced many —

Canadian decorator John Schofield Manuel designed this bedroom for the 1989 Designers Showhouse in Toronto using *Bengali*, the first wallpaper pattern Brunschwig & Fils made.

mostly French — wallpapers that had been found in historic American houses. Brunschwig also turned to historic houses and museums for wallpapers, as they had done previously with fabrics. One of the early trompe l'oeil wallpaper designs developed was found in Mrs. B. and Murray Douglas's favorite source of inspiration in Paris, the Musée des Arts Décoratifs. The document — the original block-printed design — consisted of arched and garlanded columns, clipped hedges, and the sky above; with seventeen screens it became *La Haie*. (See Carl D'Aquino's use of it in Chapter 13, p. 155.)

Historically, the first wallpapers to be made were hand-painted *(papiers peints)*, and later papers were block-printed on separate sheets. Long continuous rolls of wallpaper were not manufactured until after the mechanical advances of the nineteenth century. Nowadays Brunschwig & Fils can call upon different printing methods to suit each

Newly added to the Brunschwig wallpaper collection is *Suffield Arabesque*, which is based on a documentary wallpaper found in the Hathaway House in Suffield, Connecticut, the source of four wonderful late-eighteenth-century arabesque papers.

individual design. Some patterns are still block-printed in small ateliers, using paper with hand-painted backgrounds. These papers have great texture, but the process is labor-intensive, production quantities are necessarily small, and therefore they are expensive. They are made with stencils cut from metal or wood blocks, which are charged at an ink box and applied to the paper under a heavy press. Areas the blocks miss are filled in by hand with a paintbrush. These block-printed papers have an inexact, free look to them, but it comes at a price. Hand-printed papers are costly, and they have to be water- and soil-resistant or the gouache pigments wash away.

The closest thing to block printing by hand is hand printing on tables. For this process two printers carry a screen along the table. It is fascinating to see how the printers "skip print," printing every other repeat, and then come back and fill in the missing repeats. But no printer likes to have people come and watch, as it interferes with the printer's concentration and workday. Machine screen printing with flat or rotary screens produces excellent wallpaper, and as it is faster it helps cut the cost. As with fabrics, stripes are always printed on rotary screen machines because it is very difficult to join stripes accurately using hand-placed screens.

In the early eighteenth century, before wallpaper was in common use, many fashionable French interiors contained furniture, curtains, and walls covered en suite in the same patterned fabric. Just after the first Brunschwig wallpaper collection came out, Mrs. B. was quoted in the *Interior Decorator and Contract News:*

The use of matching fabric and wallpaper is an outgrowth of the eighteenth-century style of stretching fabric on the walls with matching fabric at the windows. Wallpaper eliminates the expense of stretching a fabric and, with the many various wallpaper grounds available today such as silk, burlap, and other artificial textures, one can achieve the same softness in appearance. Wallpapers properly chosen are ideal backgrounds for pictures. Many people ask me if it isn't disturbing to hang pictures on papered walls. To the contrary, depending on the type of pictures and the paper, it often enhances the collection.

The French have always used more fabric on walls than Americans. While American houses usually have better insulation, sometimes modern construction makes one wish for that nice, padded fabric effect.

By the late eighteenth century, during the reign of Louis XVI, there was a return to classicism in France. Meanwhile, in England, the

Using a pattern called *Four Seasons*, designer William Kulp followed the classic style of using a toile fabric en suite — with the fabric on the bed and the walls, including the closets — in Brunschwig Vice President Ross Francis's New York apartment. Many customers wanted the en suite effect, so Brunschwig & Fils reproduced many of their toile fabric patterns on wallpaper, which is easier and less laborious to apply than fabric.

Eveline Peardon selected découpage wallpaper with a *Bordure Ruban* border to create a very twentieth-century version of the "print room" fashionable in the early nineteenth century.

Adam brothers were producing classical, restrained wall decorations, fostered by the discovery of Herculaneum and Pompeii. In France the Napoleonic Empire style developed after the Revolution, inspired by the glories of ancient Rome. Today's resurgent interest in French arabesque wallpapers — neoclassic curlicues originally inspired by Arabian motifs — was sparked by an exhibition at the Cooper-Hewitt Museum in New York. This exhibit may have been inspired by one of the first wallpapers — an arabesque pattern — that the Hewitt sisters collected. English wallpapers of the time, called grotesques from the word *grotto*, incorporated Italian-inspired details such as masks and figures.

Another wall treatment popular in the early nineteenth century was découpage — cutout motifs pasted on walls to create "print rooms." Garlands, medallions, and other motifs were available, printed on paper for gentlewomen to cut out and glue in decorative patterns, forming their own, often very stylish, wall coverings. Most of these decorations were printed in grisaille, a monochrome gray or sepia. Now Brunschwig prints a wallpaper that captures the spirit of découpage, so no one has to go to all that trouble.

In the same vein is *Lunéville Plates*, a wallpaper that depicts plates hung vertically in a panel. (See Chapter 1, p. 9.) This paper was inspired by the fashion of hanging plates on the wall as decoration that started at the end of the seventeenth century when William and Mary of Orange came to the English throne from the Netherlands. They brought delft earthenware and Chinese porcelain plates that were hung by the hundreds on the walls and put on the tops of chests and armoires at Hampton Court. Hanging precious or unusual plates on the wall is still a wonderful decorative idea. Having a wallpaper with the same conceit takes the idea one step further, into a faux fantasy.

For many years Brunschwig & Fils had been intrigued by Chinese painted wallpapers, using them in repeating form as design sources for textiles such as *Volière Chinoise*, introduced in the Château Thoiry collection. One of the greatest of Chinese panoramic wallpapers is at Winterthur in the important Chinese Parlor. "In this room," Murray Douglas points out, "they change the slipcovers seasonally, which shows how versatile Chinese wallpaper can be as a background."

From the late seventeenth to the early nineteenth centuries, hand-painted Chinese papers were developed as trade goods for the European and American markets. These papers could be ordered in a variety of background colors, and customers could specify if they wanted paper

Cleveland interior decorator Donald Doskey designed this dining room using *Volière Chinoise* wallpaper, based on an eighteenth-century hand-painted Chinese wallpaper found in the Château de Thoiry. The paper depicts extravagantly drawn pheasants perched on bamboo branches, while hummingbirds fly amid morning glories and camellias.

featuring birds, pots, or scenes with pagodas and people. Customers could also order from China extra hand-painted birds and other motifs to be cut out and pasted on as they fancied. Europeans developed their own romanticized versions of Chinese papers as part of the chinoiserie style that influenced European and American decorative arts in the late eighteenth century. An interesting chinoiserie wallpaper Brunschwig developed for the Winterthur Museum, called *China Fancy*, is based on a document that combined elements of both Chinese and Indian motifs — a cross-fertilization of ideas that was probably originally hand painted in England in the mid-eighteenth century by Chinese artists imported for that purpose.

Around this time the well-to-do in America often commissioned their own murals, painted by itinerant artists, in imitation of expensive European scenic wallpapers. Subjects chosen might be scenes of family houses, landscapes, places they'd visited, or fantasy places they'd like to visit, emulating the famous French scenic papers like *Conquistadores in Peru* or *Scenes from the Bosphorus*. Scenic papers printed in a series of panels were expensive even by that time. Réveillon and Zuber were both well-known French wallpaper producers; Zuber exists to this day, producing similar panoramic scenic papers. When Mayor Edward Koch

put together a committee to restore Gracie Mansion — the handsome Federal house that is now the official residence of the Mayor of New York — committee head Albert Hadley discovered a pristine antique scenic paper in the attic of a Hudson Valley Federal house. This was installed in the Gracie Mansion's dining room. Because of their reputation for producing fine, custom-made papers, Brunschwig was commissioned to produce the rest of the wallpapers for Gracie Mansion. In the entrance hall a striped documentary paper with a border from the Cooper-Hewitt Museum was chosen. From the way the border was placed with the stripes, Brunschwig designers realized the original stripe must have been printed horizontally across the paper. Though it was far more difficult to hang than regular wallpaper because it had to be placed on the wall horizontally, it was custom-reproduced that way. Thankfully, skilled paper-hangers were able to match up the stripes accurately — no easy feat.

In 1978 Brunschwig acquired the rights to a collection of French documentary wallpapers that had been accumulated by Nancy McClelland. This was presented as the French Folio collection. It is worth noting that, of the twelve wallpapers included in the collection, ten of them are still going strong.

Wallpaper remnants are often discovered in attics. At Montgomery Place, a Hudson Valley house in New York State, a trunkful of wallpaper scraps was discovered, all in their original bright colors, which had been protected from the light. One of these patterns still dresses the walls of the grand house's drawing room (although it is somewhat faded). It has been reprinted by Brunschwig & Fils and called *Livingston*, after the New York State family connected with the house.

Flocking is a technique that was used as early as the seventeenth century, to imitate Venetian and Genoese velvet wall hangings. Flocking was created then by block-printing a design with glue and then scattering minute shearings of waste wool over it. Nowadays the shearings are generally made from synthetic fibers and the technique is mechanized. Flocking resurged in popularity in the 1940s and 1950s — until it became vulgarized by gaudy restaurants and nightclubs. Now flocking has returned on documentary designs, particularly for use in museum houses. A wallpaper document from the Society for the Preservation of New England Antiquities (SPNEA) that included flocked details inspired *Osborn Arcaded Panel*, a Brunschwig & Fils design. (See Chapter 15, p. 169.)

Artists often come to Brunschwig with wallpaper ideas. One had

Opposite: The Gracie Mansion front hall, hung with a specially commissioned documentary striped paper, made by Brunschwig & Fils based on an original in the Cooper-Hewitt Museum. Because it was discovered that the original wallpaper and its border had been printed an unorthodox way, the paper had to be hung horizontally, a far more difficult task than hanging it vertically.

During the restoration of the historic Hudson Valley house, Montgomery Place, this trunk filled with wallpaper, still vividly colored, was discovered.

Donna Lang, author of *Decorating with Paper*, treated an awkward corner in a hall by using *Bibliothèque* wallpaper in conjunction with other Brunschwig papers — cutout "plates" from *Découpage*, figures from *Battle of Valmy*, and jugs from *Country Crockery*.

the idea to do a linen-fold trompe l'oeil paper; but linen fold itself is trompe l'oeil — it's wood carved to look like stylized folded linen! So his version would have been a double trompe l'oeil. Brunschwig did not pick up this idea. But his next idea was to make Brunschwig's *Leopard* velvet pattern into a wallpaper border with a swag — and that is a best-seller. Other trompe l'oeil wallpapers include faux stone effects, such as the apparently three-dimensional *Ashlar*, found in the entrance hall at Boscobel, a historic house on the Hudson; *Secret Garden*, with its greenery climbing up a stone wall; and *Stonework*, with its simple stone blocks, found in the corridors of the Brunschwig & Fils New York offices with a Gothic border of *Stonework Arch*.

The bookshelf effect of *Bibliothèque*, designed by Richard Neas, is a pattern to have fun with, especially as some of the trompe l'oeil "books" don't have titles — giving you a chance to have a private joke and fill in your own.

Another Brunschwig & Fils trompe l'oeil wallpaper is *Mignonne* (see p. 65), based on a fragile sheet-paper document that imitates gathered, sprigged taffeta. A border was invented by Brunschwig & Fils's designers to give the design even greater credibility at the cornice, making the drapery appear to hang under a swagged valance. Though the original document was in white, several other colorways have been introduced, with cream proving the most popular.

When *Mignonne* was featured in a room photographed for *House Beautiful* and captioned quite correctly as wallpaper, readers called and wrote, insisting that someone had made a mistake — it was fabric, they said, and where could they get it? Brunschwig & Fils responded to the many requests by making a fabric that imitated the design as if it were stretched out flat. This fabric sold only moderately well. Paper is a great deal less expensive and much simpler to use than shirred, figured silk taffeta, which periodically has to be taken down and cleaned. And the real thing wasn't nearly as amusing.

Murray Douglas feels that the importance of wallpaper borders can't be stressed enough. In the early nineteenth century, what made rooms stylish were colored walls created with paint or plain paper, a stripe, or a viney type of pattern — and then a knockout border.

For instance, a room in the Harrison Gray Otis house, the Boston headquarters of the Society for the Preservation of New England Antiquities (SPNEA) has a neoclassic look that is not primarily pastels and white. It's a very rich room with yellow and turquoise green, cameos and garlands . . . and an unlikely Pompeian border. It all works wonderfully with the dark green draperies, gold trim, and black horsehair.

Present-day borders can be complex or simple. A ribbon stripe can give a bandbox neatness to a simple bedroom, outlining the doors, ceiling, and dadoes. Borders can be used to crisscross a ceiling or to outline panels, forming a picture-frame effect on the wall. A combination of several different borders at a crown molding allows the decorator to be inventive, while a border at chair-rail height gives a logical reason to use a different wallpaper for the lower part of the room. Sometimes designs are inspired by antique embroidery. Brunschwig & Fils interpreted some English crewel bed hangings found at the Winterthur Museum and transformed them into wallpaper. The decorative embroidered edge was used for a border paper called *Hare and Hound*. The border has been used in many different settings and is particularly apt for dining rooms. (It can be seen used in a kitchen in Chapter 11, p. 137.)

At the end of the nineteenth century, to counteract the glut of overly elaborate decoration, aesthetic-movement wallpapers — such as those by William Morris — became fashionable. These designs did not transform a room into a wood or a palace, but simply put a flat pattern

Trellis effects work well in solariums and garden rooms. Brunschwig's *Treillage* series of papers includes trellis sidewall, pilasters, capitals, bases, and a combination of borders. Several of these papers are seen here in a Lake Forest sun room designed by Mary Southworth of Southworth Interiors.

This 1839 illustration from *Willy's Rambles for Young Children* by Jane Marcet shows a wallpapering scene indicating that wallpaper borders — like the one being cut — were in frequent use during the nineteenth century.

on the walls. Americans seem to be going through that same feeling of restraint in the 1990s after the comparative excess of the 1980s. Monotone *toile de Jouy* designs; the wood grain–like *Teawood* (based on a Brighton Pavilion idea); the patterned-all-over *Coraux* (based on mid-nineteenth-century biological documents); and *Talavera*, a document from an upstate New York house of the same name, are some of the simple wallpapers that sell very well today. However, the more pared-down a room is, the more the details count; and the quality of everything in it has to be superb.

Murray Douglas's Top Ten Wallpapers

1. *Adirondack*. The kind of trompe l'oeil log cabin effect that makes you want to smile *and* meet the artist! (See it used by Norma Goulder Savin in Chapter 8, p. 110.)

2. *Ananas*. Medium-scaled and perfect for a country dining room, this paper was one of Nancy McClelland's eighteenth-century French finds.

3. *China Fancy*. This paper has the appeal of hand-painted Chinese watercolor papers but with a smaller, more manageable repeat for smaller areas.

4. *Debussy Moiré*. A glamorous faux moiré that looks especially effective in its darker colorways. A great background for paintings.

5. *Fisher House Floral*. Elegant garlands of roses and grapes, first seen by the Brunschwig team on a document at Winterthur. Later we discovered an unfaded piece of the same design at the Musée des Arts Décoratifs, so with Winterthur's permission, this brighter coloring gave us the colors of the design's translucent fruit.

6. *Fuchsia Trellis*. Two of my favorite elements combined in an Art Nouveau–inspired design.

7. *La Haie Panel*. For creating your very own garden or secret world. (See Carl D'Aquino's use of it in Chapter 13, p. 155.)

8. *Mignonne*. For my future tented boudoir.

9. *Spatterware*. A perfect foil for borders — timeless, reads color well, unpompous.

10. *Thérèse*. Another classic. I remember the green-and-black on white pattern in a country dining room with lots of green Wedgwood pottery and white ironstone.

Ohio designer Bruce Roberts used *Mignonne* in this hall. To achieve the trompe l'oeil effect of shirring in this wallpaper pattern, the design requires twenty-six screens, with nine different shades of gray alone (illustrated on the *gamme*, the color-patch strip in the selvedge).

Murray Douglas's Top Five Wallpaper Borders ↜

1. *Bosphore* border. All that the Napoléon III era stood for, in trompe l'oeil splendor. (See it in Murray Oliver's room for Drumsnab in Chapter 9, p. 124.)

2. *Elvire* border. The Victorian version of the above! Balmoral, here we come!

3. *Entrelacs et Pirouettes*. Block-printed by hand, architectural, rich color, complements many papers. (See it used with *Les Sylphides* in Sally Caughman's dining room for the Bishop's residence, Chapter 9, p. 116.)

4. *Tipperary* border and sidewall. The epitome of rusticity for the cottage of your dreams. (See it in Murray Douglas's guest room, Chapter 6, p. 78.)

5. *Volubilis*. Like a packet of multicolored morning glories in hybrid colors.

5

Furniture

Opposite: This *St. Charles* chair, made by Brunschwig and covered in *La Portugaise*, is in Tom and Eveline Peardon's breakfast room in Connecticut.

Overleaf: The Boston Design Center was originally the largest matériel warehouse in the world, used in World War II to store tanks and guns for shipping to Europe. Today the Design Center displays more beauty than bullets. As of October 1994 the Brunschwig & Fils furniture collection has been combined with the company's fabric, wallpaper, and trimmings display in an expanded showroom in the Center. The upholstered furniture is almost always covered in plain fabrics or nonthreatening patterns in light colors, so customers are not turned off by highly individual designs.

"Customers were continually asking us where they could get the chairs that appeared in our advertisements," says Patrick Mongiello, Brunschwig's vice president of marketing and sales, who initiated the collection of soft upholstered furniture introduced by Brunschwig & Fils in 1986. "We were pushed into making furniture."

Brunschwig & Fils furniture turned out to be a logical move. The familiar advertising copy that had appeared in all the top decorating magazines changed from "The chair is Régence, the fabric is Brunschwig" to "The fabric is Brunschwig, the chair is too."

Finding the right manufacturer was not easy. Quality was important, price secondary. "We wanted a fine product, but we needed a manufacturer who could handle volume," says Patrick Mongiello. He did not want to establish a connection in the Carolinas because of the area's reputation for mass production. Eventually a manufacturer was found on the West Coast that offered appropriate excellence plus growth capacity. Another facility was found outside Toronto and a third on the East Coast. All three make different products. Says Patrick Mongiello, "Our American customers want comfort in upholstered furniture, and that's what we emphasize. These pieces are hand-assembled on kiln-dried hardwood frames with individually placed and hand-tied coil springs. Many of the pieces are available in custom as well as conventional sizes."

"European customers are different," Patrick Mongiello admits. "They don't require comfort or quality as much as the Americans. Europeans won't buy an expensive new sofa, but they do want the Brunschwig aestheic in the fabric — a great covering. They use, however, a very different color palette, especially for the diffused light of England."

The furniture collection now numbers more than one hundred

items. Patrick's favorite piece? "The *Cavendish*. It's a good-looking roll-arm, classic sofa, a staple of the collection," he says. "And my favorite fabric is *La Portugaise*."

Other items — hard furniture such as tables, chairs, accessories, and lamps — were introduced in 1992 under the guidance of designer Lewis Paul. "These were also a natural outgrowth," Patrick Mongiello explains, "as they were needed to decorate the growing number of showrooms." In 1993 the Saratoga collection was introduced — a small selection of basic upholstered pieces of a quality similar to the regular collection but stocked in greater quantities to allow for speedier delivery.

The Brunschwig hard-frame furniture and table and lighting collections are designed for those who want traditional furniture but not necessarily real antiques. They are well made with good paintwork that looks antique. They wouldn't fool an expert, but they aren't meant to.

Lewis Paul includes in the collection a lot of painted furniture and unique objects that cannot be found anywhere else, such as footstools, a recently included dog bed, and a quartet of Regency-inspired chairs with painted backs depicting the four seasons. He has assembled a team of artists who paint furniture. "Oh yes, they can be difficult," he says, "but they're good. Too expensive, that's the problem." He looks around the world for ideas. "It's often a team effort. For instance, many of our lamps are made in Italy. The Italian suppliers make suggestions, we make suggestions, and we work it out."

Every item is carefully scrutinized by the Brunschwig furniture design team in North White Plains. "They're very lenient about ideas," Lewis Paul says. "And they're usually right — if they don't like something, it's because it's wrong!" Price? There's a limit to what people will pay, Lewis explains, except for an art object. "We have to do some degree of volume, so we don't just make reproductions. The top decorators often have their own special sources, so we don't sell great amounts to them. We appeal to the next level." Paul's job includes making the furniture collection blend sympathetically with newly added fabric and wallpaper collections. When the Russian fabric collection was introduced, for instance, he produced a lamp inspired by a Fabergé egg, and a Russian urn lamp.

6 🖋

Creating Brunschwig & Fils Collections

Every spring and fall the design studio at Brunschwig & Fils in New York creates a new collection of fabrics. Each new collection may consist of several themes, and each fabric generally comes in a range of colors. New passementerie — braids, fringes, and other trimmings — are added where needed. A book of fresh wallpapers and wallpaper borders is introduced each year. A new range of furniture, lamps, tables, and accessory collections are introduced annually, and many of these pieces are also interspersed throughout the regular collections. Another range of fabrics is constantly in development for contract work — for offices and establishments that order large quantities. A growing segment of the business handles fabrics for hotels, health care facilities, restaurants, and other public areas. And Brunschwig & Fils always includes a collection of less expensive fabrics designed for informal summer houses, growing families, or young couples who appreciate Brunschwig style but are just starting to feather their nests.

All these collections are found in the Brunschwig & Fils New York offices, which spread over two floors of the Decoration and Design Building in Manhattan — known familiarly as the D & D. And Brunschwig showrooms across America and throughout the world also display new fabric, wallpaper, and furniture collections.

Within each Brunschwig & Fils fabric collection a special theme is developed, sometimes based on patterns newly designed by talented artists, or sometimes on documentary patterns from a museum or a historic house. Translating original hand-painted textiles into printed cloth requires the most exquisite skill and a thorough understanding of

The restaurant at the Jonathan Club, a private men's club in downtown Los Angeles, was designed by Logan Brown using *Royal Promenade* panel wallpaper in a specially ordered color.

the painting process. To create Brunschwig's *Palampore*, a pattern based on a *palampore* at the Royal Ontario Museum (see Chapter 1, p. 10), detailed photographs of the original document were used to see how best to make the pattern appear painted by hand. Working with the actual document is far superior to working from a photograph, no matter how detailed. But many museums will not allow documents to be removed, so engravers sometimes visit the documents on-site. The *Palampore* design project took two years to complete. The original palampore was eventually interpreted in several ways: as a complete panel, using the border as a stripe, and using the rock and earth formations as an extremely successful all-over pattern.

One of the first museums that Brunschwig & Fils worked with was the Museum of Early Southern Decorative Arts (MESDA), located in the restored village of Old Salem, North Carolina. Together with museum director Frank Horton, Zelina Brunschwig and Murray Douglas found an eighteenth-century embroidered woman's tie-on pocket, with a slit for the hand on the outside. On its underside was a sophisticated striped and figured late-eighteenth-century block-printed textile similar to European woven stripes of the period. A pattern called *Salem Tavern Stripe* was developed for use in the Innkeeper's House in Old Salem and put into the Brunschwig & Fils MESDA collection. Later it was discovered that the woman's pocket had belonged to the great-great-grandmother of Brunschwig's vice president of development, Ross Johnson Francis. From MESDA, Ross Francis also developed a very close reproduction of wool *moreen*, a fabric used in many early American houses that can now be specially ordered.

Zelina Brunschwig's and Murray Douglas's first source of inspiration as students in Paris had been the Musée des Arts Décoratifs, so naturally they were thrilled to be invited to use the museum's design resources. The Brunschwig team hoped to develop a printed version of a sumptuous brocaded silk, preferably of the Louis XV period because they needed a rococo design. It seemed that everything they were shown had already been adapted, but they finally found a pathetic, threadbare piece of brocade that had lost much of its warp and most of its brocading weft. A faint pattern of ribbons, roses, and the roots of rose trees could just be made out. The team felt it had the makings of a wonderful design. It became part of the collection as *Rivoli*. "What is so lovely about adapting brocades is that they have already been taken through the simplification process, because they were designed for weaving," says Murray Douglas. "You get down to the essence of the

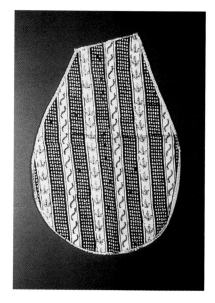

From the design on the underside of a woman's tie-on pocket found in the Museum of Early Southern Decorative Arts in Winston-Salem, Brunschwig & Fils developed *Salem Tavern Stripe*. The design is probably of French derivation, in light of the fleur-de-lys motif. This American block print used madder dye, which can run the gamut from aubergine through red to pink, depending on the mordant used.

idea. What you lose in the printing process is the reflective quality of silk — the light and shade — the glamorous silky look. But you can give it a glaze if you want it to glow, or a matte appearance by printing on linen, and still keep the design. You would never put silk into a country room, but the design itself works well in a rural setting."

Probably Brunschwig's most successful museum relationship has been with the Henry Francis du Pont Winterthur Museum. Over the years, many designs have been developed from Winterthur documents. "The success of the Winterthur collaboration has been in our care in selection and in our being faithful to the originals," says Murray Douglas.

As a design student Murray Douglas studied the Royal Pavilion at Brighton — the prince regent's marine villa extravaganza, constructed in England between 1815 and 1822 — and was enormously intrigued: "I've always felt it was an interior designer's dream, and absolutely mad," she says. Later she came across the John Nash watercolors of the royal getaway, exhibited at the Cooper-Hewitt Museum in New York. Nash was the architect responsible for the oriental look of the pavilion, though the core structure, a simpler, Palladian villa, was by architect Henry Holland. Through Cooper-Hewitt, Mrs. Douglas got to know Brighton Pavilion's enthusiastic director, John Morley, enabling Brunschwig & Fils to make a Brighton Pavilion collection. Four large panels of a mural in the Long Corridor were adapted as wallpaper, and a companion glazed chintz, *Royal Glade*, turned out to be a best-seller.

Not only was Brighton Pavilion full of chinoiserie and Moorish decorations, it also had faux bois in fantastic colors. A wood-grained

Murray Douglas initiated a Brunschwig collection inspired by England's Royal Pavilion at Brighton. This included the firm's first really large wallpaper panels, *Royal Promenade*, adapted by artist John Jacoby from murals in the Royal Pavilion's pink-and-blue Corridor.

This watercolor of the Royal Pavilion at Brighton, an oriental fantasy designed for the prince regent, is by its creator, John Nash.

The oldest paper at the bottom of a "sandwich" of wallpapers found at Talavera, New York, inspired a new wallpaper design, a linen print, and a silk warp design.

This is the document from the Henry Francis du Pont Winterthur Museum in Delaware upon which Brunschwig & Fils based the toile *Bird and Thistle*.

pattern called *Teawood* inspired by the Brighton Pavilion became part of the Brunschwig Royal Pavilion collection. It turned out to be the classic forerunner of many grained and striéd papers and fabrics that were later added to the line. (An example of *Teawood* in a natural wood-grain coloring can be seen in Chapter 1, p. 20. A fantastic, unnatural blue colorway of the design is shown in Chapter 7, p. 92.)

A single design idea is frequently developed into both a textile and a wallpaper; one such popular pattern is *Talavera*, named after a handsome 1820 house near the Hudson River in New York State. This house has belonged to the same family for many years. Its owner, Mrs. J. Van Ness Philip, invited Mrs. Douglas to visit, with a view toward commissioning a wallpaper replacement. When she asked for a sample of the damaged wallpaper from the grand-scaled reception room, the owner reached up and ripped off a whole piece. "I realized immediately that it was a sandwich of papers, going down to the original plaster," she says. Very carefully the six layers of wallpaper were peeled apart. All except the very earliest had borders. The last, a pattern of pale, decorative palmlike leaves, was the design Brunschwig & Fils put in their collection, as both paper and fabric. Now it is once again being used in the house for which it was named. The other papers have not yet been used, but may be. A study of their styles provides a fascinating interior design history of the house.

A popular Brunschwig & Fils English copperplate pattern, called *Bird and Thistle*, was originally found in a red colorway, looking pristine and glorious on a bed in the Franklin Room in the Winterthur Museum. Mrs. Douglas knew it would be a wonderful design to reproduce, but Winterthur could only loan a badly faded blue piece for Brunschwig to work with. The design team had to commission an artist to redraw and reconstruct what they surmised to be the full design, because the remnant was missing its edges. This took time. "Normally, if you have good original fragments — or documents, as they're called — you can be pretty accurate," said Murray Douglas. "We did the best we could, and it's not bad, but it could have been better. The sad thing is that a couple of months after we reproduced it, I found an unblemished piece of the documentary fabric — in the red coloring we had wanted — at the estate sale of a man who had been in the screen print business. He'd collected many documentary fabrics and lived only about a mile from my country house! What a shame we didn't find it sooner, but the pattern has been wonderfully popular."

Occasionally a documentary design is adopted that does require changing, such as this appealing Japanese design called *Shimo*, originally of kimono-clad white rats. The design team knew Americans would never warm to rats, so they turned them into white rabbits!

Above, right: This bathroom was designed by Patrick Willoughby of David Zinnerman for a Georgian mansion in Lincolnshire, England. The *Shimo* wallpaper — with white rabbits instead of rats — was chosen because it blended with existing 1960s orange bathroom fixtures.

In every collection, Brunschwig likes to include a "conversational" design. This can range from purely spectacular to whimsical patterns or even, as Murray Douglas says, "something nutty." The intent is to surprise, amuse, and get the adrenaline flowing. A dramatic wallpaper based on a Korean screen fits this category, as does *Shimo*, a droll design of rabbits dressed in kimonos.

Putting together a collection comprising a variety of fabrics and papers is a complex business involving many people and sometimes taking several years. Fortunately textiles used for decoration are generally less prone to the vagaries of fashion than are clothing materials — though it is surprising to look back over the years and see how color preferences have changed from decade to decade. For instance, *Chinese Blossoms*, one of Billy Baldwin's favorite chintzes, was originally produced in soft colorings. In the 1960s the design sold best in bright colors on a black ground. In the 1990s decorators prefer it again in the original soft-colored version, reflecting its painted wallpaper origins. (See Chapter 12, p. 144, for Bill Bennette's use of *Chinese Blossoms*.)

The French Château Collection 🖋

The Renaissance Château de Thoiry-en-Yvelines, twenty-five miles west of Paris, was completed in 1564 and is renowned for its architectural eccentricity. It was built for an aristocrat by an alchemist-architect and sited so that, at the summer and winter solstice, the sun appears to rise or set in the Grand Vestibule. The windows are canted so you can see light flooding through the house.

The young Vicomte Paul de la Panouse, owner of the Château de Thoiry-en-Yvelines, married Annabelle, a beautiful American girl from Minneapolis. In exchange for a royalty arrangement to help with its upkeep, she gave Brunschwig the run of the château to choose from among European and Asian documents spanning three hundred years.

On the grounds is a safari park of elephants, tigers, zebras, and other animals that roam freely through a natural landscape of forest and lakes. Walking in the woods one can hear lions roaring, so it is not surprising that animals figure in quite a few of the fabrics that were developed. A Bengali folk-art wood panel was found in the master bedroom depicting antelopes, birds, snakes, and tigers in a stylized landscape; this was adapted into *Tapisserie*, a fabric and a wallpaper border. Annabelle used this print to reupholster a charming antique dog's bed in the château. An eighteenth-century Chinese hand-painted wallpaper — of pheasants on bamboo branches twined with morning glories and camellias — became a cotton print and companion paper called *Volière Chinoise*. (See it in Chapter 4, p. 59, and Chapter 7, p. 90). The entrance hall of the château is in shades of heavenly blue, and the interior is filled with light pouring through the enfilade of rooms. One of them, the White Salon, has a harpsichord embellished with rococo *singeries* decorations by Jean-Baptiste Huet, the French artist who not only designed genre scene toiles for Oberkampf but also painted chinoiserie panels in many small *cabinets* — tiny, private lacquered rooms often used for displaying precious objects — for French ladies of style. Brunschwig & Fils used Huet's decoration, which shows costumed monkeys making music and play-acting, for both wallpaper and fabric. The pattern is called *Les Scapins* ("mischievous ones"). (See it in use in Chapter 12, p. 140.)

Murray Douglas was prowling behind the boiseries of a room at Thoiry — boiseries are installed in such a way that a narrow walkway exists between wood and wall — when she spotted a rag that had been tucked up long ago on one of the supports, probably by a housemaid. A madraslike plaid, this chance find was developed into a woven fabric

This page from the Thoiry scrapbook shows the château on the day of the summer solstice, reflected in its lake. Beside it is the Bengali wood panel document upon which *Tapisserie* border was based. The middle picture shows a detail of the satin curtain panels embroidered in silk and chenille in the eighteenth century by Angélique, a great-great-grandmother of the family. From this staggering amount of handwork Brunschwig & Fils developed a chintz pattern with a border, *Fleurs d'Angélique*. Though the chintz doesn't have the three-dimensional look of the original chenille embroidery shown here, the design is effective. The bottom pictures show a photograph of the walls in one of Thoiry's great rooms, covered in an exuberant and amazingly preserved pattern of seventeenth-century embossed and gilded leather scrollwork called *Aristoloche*. Brunschwig produces the design on linen and, more daringly, in red and gold on lamé Jacquard made in a Swiss mill. This fabric was used by Bill Blass to make glamorous evening skirts. Next to it is a watercolor by Murray Douglas showing the lamé version of *Aristoloche* on cushions in a romantic setting.

Thoiry at dawn - Summer Solstice

painted panel, document for Tapisserie

embroidery detail - Fleurs d'Angelique

late 17th c. embossed leather walls

MBD watercolor - Aristoloche

called *Clémence*. Even more serendipitous was finding a real, painted *indienne* fragment on a chair in the attic. This was adapted into a cotton print called *Compagnie des Indes*, after the mercantile company that probably brought it from India. Sitting in the middle of the chair was a bird's nest that had fallen from the rafters, for there were sizable holes in the roof. Keeping up a great house is not easy, but since then the dynamic Vicomtesse has initiated a "buy a shingle" campaign to help reroof Thoiry.

The Cottage Orné Collection 🐦

Marie Antoinette was not the only one lured by the fanciful idea of rural life when she played at being a shepherdess in *Le Hameau*, a cottage built for her near the palace at Versailles. By the nineteenth century sophisticated urban French were retreating to their *petites fermes* or *manoirs*, Russians were escaping to their country *dachas*, and even stolid Queen Victoria headed for Balmoral in the Highlands, for Scotland had not only been tamed but by then was thoroughly romanticized.

One of Mrs. Douglas's favorite projects was the Cottage Orné collection, designed in conjunction with Irish designer Sybil Connolly, who steered the Brunschwig team to a picturesque thatch-roofed cottage in County Tipperary. Built in 1817 by the earl of Glengall — rumored for his lady-love — this rural retreat is a jewel of early-nineteenth-century romantic architecture. Local lore says that the cottage was the work of Regency architect John Nash, mentioned above as creator of the Royal Pavilion at Brighton. The cottage is now owned by the Irish Government and open to the public. Brunschwig was invited to collaborate with Sybil Connolly in the research and re-creation of fabrics and wallpapers of the period for use in decorating the cottage.

None of the original decoration existed, so Sybil Connolly was particularly anxious to use an early toile — copperplate printed cotton — she had discovered in the National Museum in Dublin. It was printed in an area called Balls Bridge in 1765, earlier than any documented toiles printed in England or France. Wallpapers were also needed for the house, so Mrs. Douglas dug around in the Brunschwig archives and found the perfect trompe l'oeil rustic grape-leaf border, to be complemented by an Empire-style "snowflake" of leaves in keeping with the romantic spirit of the early nineteenth century.

A guest room in the Douglas's country house is decorated with *Tipperary* side-wall and border from the Cottage Orné collection. Curtains of *New Richmond Dimity* with *Christina* fringe made up of hand-tied tassels.

Choosing *Lily of Galtee* from the Cottage Orné collection, June G. Ashton of Chicago designed this bathroom for a house in Lake Forest with elegant bordered draperies. It adjoins a dressing room decorated in the same print.

The Cottage Orné collection was taken one step further at a party that both Mrs. Douglas and Sybil Connolly were asked to attend in Atlanta. For the Swan House Ball, a big Irish-theme event held in a marquee to benefit the Atlanta Historical Society, the documentary *Dublin* toile was printed in a special green colorway to decorate the tables. The chandeliers chosen were pretty but turned out to be too small for the huge tent. So Susan Withers, the designer, cleverly had cages built around them, wrapped them in ivy, and put little lights on them. The size of the chandeliers was immediately doubled and the party was beautifully illuminated.

In a wonderful old printing mill archive in the north of England they found a group of designs dating back to the 1830s that fitted the image of the cottage perfectly. Small-scaled and informal, these patterns featured flowers, trellises, and climbing ivy.

Sybil Connolly's favorite flower was lily of the valley, so a design called *Lily of Galtée* was included in the collection.

The climbing roses and honeysuckle of Brunschwig's evocative *Sara Jane* chintz gave the cottage a romantic, Jane Austen–esque simplicity that complemented the intricacies of the cottage's whimsical Gothick architecture (see Glossary). A Swiss nineteenth-century block print called *St. Lucia*, composed of hummingbirds and roses, was equally at home in the cottage.

When the fabric patterns were all ready to be used, but the restoration of the cottage not yet finished, Mrs. Douglas painted a series of watercolors showing how the Brunschwig textiles might look in various rooms. "As I had been there I had a feeling for the house, and it was really fun — instant décor! There was no bathroom, so I turned one of

Situated in a vast park near Cahir, County Tipperary, is the 1817 Cottage Orné that inspired a Brunschwig & Fils collection. Here is a watercolor by Murray Douglas of the cottage's dining room: The tableskirt and two cushions on the window banquette are made of an English glazed chintz called *Erin*.

Opposite: In this watercolor of a bedroom in the Cottage Orné, Murray Douglas shows *Ivy Orné* glazed chintz and border on a bed and as a tableskirt on the balcony table. The wallpaper and border are of the same pattern.

the rooms into a bathroom, using the border of the trellis design and sticking the bathtub in the middle. Sybil Connolly wanted the toile to be used en suite in the bedroom, but knowing how difficult it is to paint a whole wall with a pattern, I cheated and made the bed *à la Polonaise* with toile drapery. I covered those walls with an easier-to-depict tiny stripe instead."

Brunschwig also decorated an American Gothick residence, the charming Delameter House in Rhinebeck, New York, built by American architect Alexander Jackson Davis. Designer Carolyn Guttilla created settings for the entry hall, front and back porches, a sitting room, and a bedroom, all in a cozy, unpretentious mood. Rather than imitating serious Gothic — dark and tinged with medieval religious overtones — the Delameter House became soft, warm, and personal.

The Russian Collection ❧

In 1991 a representative from the Moscow State Historical Museum approached the Brunschwig design team with a view to using documents from the Moscow museum for a collection. The liaison was Dr. David Segal, who was currently negotiating with the Metropolitan Museum to license documentary Russian jewelry and scarfs. From start to finish it took three years for the Russian collection to be developed and presented to Brunschwig customers.

Stimulated by the idea from the start, the troika of Murray Douglas, Ross Francis, and Paul Dobrowolski prudently decided not to commit themselves to anything until they visited the museum in Russia and saw exactly what was being offered. Arriving in Moscow, they discovered that the textiles and costume department of the State Historical Museum had been moved from the city's center to a building overlooking a state military prison (which happened to be a picturesque place frequently used as a background by filmmakers). Inside, the team got busy with their own cameras, photographing everything of interest in a highly organized way — one was the note-taker, one took photographs with a 35-millimeter camera, one took Polaroids. They drew and measured each pattern so as later to be able to visualize the scale of each design. The Russian curators were impressed, acknowledging that the Brunschwig team was more thorough than European firms. They were especially friendly because they had worked with Brunschwig's archivist Judy Straeten on the Russian Costume exhibition at the Metropolitan Museum in New York City. The Russians themselves were currently working on a traveling show and "tended to keep much of the good stuff they were planning to exhibit under wraps," says Mrs. Douglas. By careful sleuthing and persistence, the team was able to see and eventually use some of this special material. "We explained that we might translate their brocades into prints, but would not make any final decisions till we were back home, where we could work from slides," says Paul. They saw wonderful peasant costumes; however, it is very difficult to achieve a handmade look with a commercial product. Following the reforms of Peter the Great, most of Russian society, both peasants and aristocrats, remained true to Russian dress — such as the *sarafan*, a dress with a high waist, worn over a blouse and with a high headdress. They were also shown fabric designs from the 1920s, including a design on cloth depicting a fabulous workers-of-the world-unite icebreaking boat with two Russian flags, but decided that this design was not quite in the Brunschwig style.

One of the most Russian of all the designs in the Russian collection is this intricate, striped wool-and-tapestry weave shawl over-decorated with paisley flowers. It was designed by a renowned early-nineteenth-century craftswoman, Nadezhda Merlina. Handwoven using thirty colors, and completely reversible, this quality of shawl could cost as much as twenty thousand gold rubles at the time. It inspired *Kapli*, a striped cotton fabric.

While more refined than the country dacha, the Russian city residence never completely lost the Slavic affection for provincial comforts. Fashioned after Pushkin's study, Richard Keith Langham contrived this library for a Brunschwig brochure, using a mixture of Brunschwig fabrics and furniture and Russian antiques: a shawl of *Kapli* striped cotton print, Brunschwig's *Albert* chair covered in mohair figured velvet, a *Calliope* base with desktop, and a *Directoire Bouillotte* lamp.

Meanwhile Dr. Segal spent most of his day searching for food, because there was nowhere nearby to have lunch. Though he had the advantage of having U.S. dollars, he had to pay two people to watch the car while food-hunting. Once back at their hotel the team spread out their Polaroids and started to make selections. Moscow was going through hardships at the time — the attempted coup against Gorbachev took place within a month of their visit — and the lights would suddenly go off or the water cease flowing.

As they progressed they learned which characteristics were essentially Russian — fabulous Russian brocades, for instance, had dark colorings with black outlining and ermine tails as details. Eastern Russian textiles tended to be dramatic, three-dimensional, and generally less naturalistic than the light, delicate French brocaded silks, but as Catherine the Great had visited the silk mills of Lyons, from the eighteenth century on French and Italian influences were discernible. In the nineteenth century there were at least a hundred sophisticated weaving mills around Moscow, and today there are still small "dacha industries" doing skilled restoration work.

The Mount Vernon collection includes the *Martha Washington* print, inspired by a gold-figured silk reputedly used for her wedding dress. Shown here is the original document.

The Mount Vernon Collection

Mount Vernon has always been one of Murray Douglas's favorite American museum houses, perhaps because an ancestor, Miss Harriet Comegys, was one of the early regents of the Mount Vernon Ladies' Association, which purchased the house in 1858 to save it from disintegration. Over the years Brunschwig & Fils has provided the house with reproduction textiles. It is one of the most accurately restored of museum houses due to the existence of careful inventories and correspondence relating to its furnishings. So when the house's curator, Christine Meadows, and Hickory Furniture approached Brunschwig & Fils to work with them to create a special Mount Vernon collection of decorative fabrics, it was a natural fit.

George and Martha Washington's two-story wood mansion on the Potomac was built on land granted to John Washington, great-grandfather of George, in 1674. George Washington's father, Augustine, resided there with his young family, and George's older half-brother, Lawrence, settled on the property when he married. He named it Mount Vernon, after Admiral Edward Vernon, under whom he had served in the Caribbean. After Lawrence's death, George acquired the property by lease from his widow in 1754; he inherited it in 1761, following her death.

After George married the wealthy widow Martha Dandridge Custis in 1759, many new furnishings were ordered for the house. Most were bought through Washington's London agent, who also sold tobacco produced on the plantation. Washington's furniture and decorating orders, in his own hand, survive today. His favorite paint colors — the most expensive of the time — were Prussian blue and verdigris, which he noted as being "grateful to the eye." As Gouverneur Morris of Philadelphia wrote to Washington, "I think it of great Importance to fix the Taste of our country properly, and I think your example will go very far in that Respect." After the American Revolution, when Washington's taste was closely observed, he patronized American cabinetmakers for Mount Vernon and used French furniture in his New York residence. He himself described his taste in furniture as "neat and fashionable."

Fabrics in the collection include *Mount Vernon Plantation Toile*, an "invented" toile created from period engravings of the house and garden interspersed with garlands, and *Washington Crest Damask*, which includes Washington's family motto, *Exitus acta probat*, "The end proves the deed."

The toile on this bed shows an example of an authorized inspiration, a present day–designed toile using motifs that relate to Mount Vernon, the historic house where George Washington lived. The design was made in five colors and was also made into a wallpaper.

Working with historic houses or museums is a learning experience. Special arrangements are negotiated with each historic association, usually to pay a royalty or to provide fabric for restoration, but every case is different. Sometimes a museum will approach Brunschwig & Fils because of its reputation for producing fine products. Sometimes Brunschwig goes to a museum, with the hope of finding an unusual document. The final results will not appear until many meetings, paintings of repeats, strike-offs of colorways in the print factories, and hours of work have taken place. There are three ways to work with museum documents. An *authorized reproduction* is as close in design to the original as is possible, with virtually no change in scale, design, color, intrinsic fiber, weave, or manufacturing method; an *authorized adaptation* is similar to the above, but uses contemporary

Julie Perin Bird — daughter of Mrs. B.'s friend, decorator Jane Perin — designed this room for the 1993 Southport Decorator Showhouse using fabrics from the Brunschwig En Vacances collection. The John Botz design *Marché aux Fleurs* is used for the curtains and sofa. Also shown is *Antigua* cotton-and-linen check in blue and white and the Chinese fish *Canton* cotton print, seen on the curtains through the door. (For other uses of John Botz designs see Chapter 13, p. 157, and Chapter 14, p. 162.)

manufacturing methods. There are some resultant compromises, but the finished product is close enough to the original to be used in a museum room setting. A design *inspired* by a document allows for many changes; but the scale remains constant, as does the spirit of the design.

Royalties are paid to museums on every yard of fabric or roll of wallpaper sold. They amount to substantial sums if sales are good, so it is in everyone's interest to pick a design that will have a long life in the collection. Through long experience, the design studio can spot patterns that will maintain their integrity and appeal to the interior design community.

Not every collection is based on museum documentary fragments, though a collection is usually designed around a theme. Clean, crisp, contemporary patterns are designed by gifted present-day artists and developed into collections that fit right into households of the 1990s. One such design was based on the fruit and flower markets of sunny Provence and southern California, sparking a popular collection called *En Vacances*. This collection ranges from simple checks to a Matisse-like print of pots of flowers to a print of lemons set between sea blue stripes, all invoking the clear, lighthearted colors of both the Mediterranean and the Pacific.

Here is a page from a Brunschwig & Fils mailing showing how fabrics, wallpapers, and trimmings can be assembled into a scheme, together with suggestions for suitable accessories.

Whatever the source of a design, each pattern must be scrutinized for all possible uses, and each collection must be balanced to include large and small prints, stripes, checks, wovens, a theme "conversation print," coordinating trimmings, wallpapers, and borders. The whole package must be "schemed," as Mrs. B. would say, so that every item justifies its ultimate use for curtains, sofa fabric, side chairs, cushions, and so forth.

Finally, once the fabrics are produced, samples are cut and hung in the showrooms with swatches of complementary possibilities attached to suggest ideas. "For many decorators, the job is done for them," stated decorator Jane Perin, who was a friend of Zelina Brunschwig. "No fabric house put it together like that before her!" Lest anyone think "scheming" is merely a help for novice designers, Brunschwig's showroom manager and staff used to enjoy seeing Billy Baldwin, standing on tiptoe, taking down the numbers of suggested coordinating fabrics!

No wonder Brunschwig showrooms, where everything is displayed to the trade, are so large. They would be even larger if a regular culling of fabrics didn't take place. Decisions to discontinue are usually based on sales, breaking the hearts of quite a few decorators, customers, and textile designers along the way. Fortunately retired fabrics are stashed in the Brunschwig archives, ready — as often happens — to be resurrected in the future.

Overleaf: In a faultless, tour-de-force bedroom for the 1985 Kips Bay Designer Showhouse, New York decorator Mario Buatta played *Verrières* off against a Nancy Lancaster–inspired lacy white bed dressed in *Richmond Dimity.*

*F*abric, wallpaper, trimming, and furniture remain static until used in actual rooms. Skilled interior designers can add another dimension to these products, bringing them to life. Each designer has his or her own style and vision with which to delight, surprise, astound, charm, and inspire. Included in the following pages is something for everyone interested in Brunschwig style.

Starting with entrance halls, and working through interior spaces of houses and apartments, a variety of photographed rooms follows, with the designers and Brunschwig products identified. Large and small, opulent and simple, town and country, private and commercial, these spaces give a wide-ranging look at the many different decorating styles of today.

Most of the photographs are of real living spaces, in France, England, Scotland, Canada, and all over America. Though general trends in interior decoration are universal, it is always interesting to note national and regional distinctions. Brunschwig & Fils echoes the world around it, to provide customers with the necessary tools to satisfy their tastes. The Brunschwig look is rooted in exemplary designs, both woven and printed, from the past, and on this firm ground the company builds designs for the present and future. While Brunschwig & Fils provides decorating materials for many grand, historic houses, it is also aware of the current inclination toward smaller houses, which are increasingly furnished with robust woven fabrics that have a controlled, intellectual, somewhat austere effect reflecting today's sensibilities.

Many of the following illustrations are of designers' own homes, revealing an accurate picture of their style. Some are from showhouses, reflecting current trends and providing designers a chance to show their skill. For understandable reasons, few client names are revealed. ≤

Rooms

7

Halls

The tone of a house or apartment is set by its entrance, whether it's a tiny passage with no more than a coat closet and a place to dump wet umbrellas or it's one of the largest rooms in the house, convertible into a salon for special occasions.

A hall is often a place to use unusual or novel wallpaper rather than vast amounts of fabric. Frequently there are few windows to curtain, and what furniture there is tends to be of the unupholstered variety. A hall or lobby is perfect for "conversational" wallpaper, such as *Bibliothèque* — a trompe l'oeil of bookshelves designed for Brunschwig by the late Richard Neas, seen here in a Donna Lang–designed house. (See Chapter 4, p. 62.) Wallpaper that might be too busy for rooms where more time is spent can make a hall spectacular.

Opposite: Designer V. Benson Small of Bittners in Louisville chose the yellow-ground colorway of Brunschwig's Chinese-inspired wallpaper *Volière Chinoise* (see also Chapter 4, p. 59) to complement the wrought-iron staircase, classical niche, and fantasy-grained floor in this stair hall in a house in Harrod's Creek, Kentucky.

Right: For this hall in a New York apartment, Los Angeles designer Ron Collier used Brunschwig's *Tenture Flottante*, a wallpaper that imitates classic Roman draped fabric, emphasized by masculine architectural drawings and a parquet floor. The chair backs seen in the dining room at the end of the hall are done in *Matteo* tapestry.

Sally Harmon Caughman of Pulliam-Morris chose Brunschwig's *La Scala* wallpaper for this hallway in the Charleston residence of the Roman Catholic bishop of South Carolina. (She was commissioned to restore the historic house after extensive damage from Hurricane Hugo.) The wallpaper design by the late Charles Tausch is based on imberlines, silk fabrics with woven striped grounds and large damask patterns, used from the eighteenth century on for upholstery and wall hangings. The pier table — sometimes called a petticoat table — and cane side chairs are some of the original furnishings of the house.

Above, right: Eveline Peardon used the sophisticated fantasy wood-grain wallpaper *Teawood,* from the Brunschwig's Royal Pavilion collection, in a naive way in this little upstairs hallway in the Peardon's Connecticut farmhouse, where the walls had been built to accommodate the essential fireplace chimney.

The halls of grand New York apartments often have black-and-white checkerboard marble floors; good hall chairs pushed up against the walls; some kind of serious case furniture, like a grandfather clock; an antique table for keys and mail; or a piece of sculpture. Large halls may include decorative architectural elements — columns, pilasters, crown molding, or overhead lanterns or chandeliers. A simple bold stripe with a contrasting border is effective, such as the specially commissioned documentary stripe used in the hall at Gracie Mansion, the official residence of New York's mayor. (See Chapter 4, p. 60.) Others prefer geometrics, abstracts, tiny all-overs, or large repeats. Chinese-inspired wallpaper always flatters good antiques and traditional furnishings — as seen in V. Benson Small's stair hall using *Volière Chinoise.* (See p. 90. The paper can also be seen in a dining room in Chapter 4, p. 59.) To really wow guests as they enter the door, trompe l'oeil drapery wallpaper can be effective, as in Ron Collier's hall papered with *Tenture Flottante* (p. 91). Wallpaper that brings the outdoors inside, such as scenics, hedges, or boscages (like the stair hall in Keith Irvine's country house, p. 93) can make a strong statement.

A wallpaper called *Forêt Foliage* imitates a tapestry of a wooded glade. Here decorator Keith Irvine, of the New York firm Irvine & Fleming, uses it not only on the walls but also on the ceiling. In the foreground, structural columns are faux fantasy palm trees, painted by coauthor Chippy Irvine. On the settee, amid satin, patchwork, and antique needlepoint cushions, can be seen the Brunschwig prints *Sun, Moon, and Stars* (also in Chapter 1, pp. 21–22) and *Les Touches* (also in Chapter 9, p. 119).

In duplexes and houses, halls frequently have the added dimension of a staircase. Wallpaper can be an important part of the background, aiding the transition between floors.

Even the most unpretentious country entrance can be enhanced by a suitable wallpaper, whether it's one that amusingly imitates wood grain, such as *Teawood* (used in a fantasy blue color for the Peardon's upstairs hall in their Connecticut farmhouse, p. 92), or the Neas design *Go With the Grain*, or even a faux log cabin wallpaper like *Adirondack* (seen in Chapter 8, p. 110).

8 🪶

Living Rooms

The exemplary living room is warm and inviting, a place for friends and family to sit, talk, play games, or read. In the past living rooms — or parlors, as they were once called — were often rather formal and prim, used only for special occasions or when guests arrived. Many nineteenth-century American houses had double parlors — one for women, one for men — with sliding or "pocket" doors between them. Living rooms in England are often called sitting rooms, and rather grander ones are drawing rooms (the room to which one "withdraws"). A really grand room might be called a salon,

Opposite: As an example of Midwestern grandeur, Ohio designer Donald Doskey designed this "great room" for a family in a Cleveland suburb using curtains of *Fleurs d'Angélique*, a pattern developed for the Château collection from curtains found in the château at Thoiry. (See Chapter 6, pp. 76–77.) In the foreground is Brunschwig's *Portuguese* tea table. The *Régence* chairs have *Arc-en-ciel* plaid backs, and the *Derby* urn lamp has a shade of Brunschwig silk.

Right: This New York living room, designed by Irvine & Fleming in the 1970s and used successfully for entertaining, has *Le Lac* as a key chintz with *Montabert taffetas* stripe, *Orientalia* print, and *Harrow* damask as complementary accents.

For Diana Vreeland's famous "garden in hell" room, Billy Baldwin used *Colombo*, a vivid nineteenth-century adaptation of an earlier *indienne* chintz. By the time this design came about, fabric printers had begun to make these patterns in repeats instead of panels.

particularly if it is used to entertain importantly and frequently. These terms are also used in America. Mrs. B., for instance, referred to the "drawing room" in her New York apartment, but the "living room" in her less formal country house.

Nowadays we like our living rooms to be useful, all-purpose spaces, with comfortable upholstered or slipcovered sofas and armchairs; plenty of attractive, luxurious down-filled cushions; curtains to soften the windows and protect the upholstery from the light; side tables to hold well-placed lamps with stylish shades; coffee tables for books, magazines, and collected objects; interesting or antique area rugs, often on top of simple geometric carpeting or sisal (or if *very* grand, on *parquet de Versailles*); a table for games; and perhaps a desk for writing. If the house has a fireplace, it will most probably be found in the living room. When unlit, this space was traditionally filled with a painted or wallpapered fire board.

Despite our increasingly casual way of life, the living room is still the place of greatest show, reflecting the taste and status of the owner. *Vogue* editor Diana Vreeland can be seen reclining on a sofa in a room she told Billy Baldwin she wanted to look like a garden, but a "garden in hell." He swathed her Manhattan drawing room in red *Colombo*. Living rooms are where the use of fabric — whether traditional cotton chintz or exuberant, luxurious silk and velvet or simple, neutral-colored textured cloth — is a necessity.

Because of the array of furniture in a living room, wallpapers may be simple or nonexistent. If the owner collects paintings, they may be displayed here, where they can be seen and enjoyed at leisure. There are differing schools of thought about the display of paintings against wallpapers; many fine-art owners get nervous at the idea of wallpaper as a background, but a good decorator knows how to find a wallpaper to enhance art in an insouciant, sophisticated way that improves the room as a whole rather than drawing too much obvious attention to the frightfully important art!

Living room furniture displays fabric flatteringly, because it is stretched over sofas, armchairs, and ottomans, displaying the design on the cloth at its best. The classic arrangement in the second half of the twentieth century consists of a sofa, loaded with cushions; small tables, sometimes circular and skirted, with lamps on either side; a coffee table in front; two upholstered armchairs with cushions at either end; an ottoman, perhaps; and several pull-up chairs with harder seats. There are endless variations on this theme, and living room furniture can

New York designer Victoria Hagan designed this 1990 Kips Bay Showhouse room to look young, modern, and rather loftlike. The furniture is spare and quirky with a postmodern touch. The fabrics are woven textures rather than prints and include Brunschwig's green-and-gold silk *Raphael* damask from Italy and, on the sofa, flax-and-cotton *Bondy* texture from France.

Using the green-striped trompe l'oeil wallpaper *Cap d'Antibes* as a background, Los Angeles designer John Cole has created a cool living area for sunny California. Fabrics used in the setting include *Ivy Madras* lace, *Toile d'Anjou*, *Périgueux* stripe, and *St. Michel* damask.

include anything from a supremely designed, never-yet-improved-on eighteenth-century fauteuil to an elegant early-nineteenth-century recamier or a comfortable late-Victorian tufted sociable; but all these pieces require some sort of upholstery or else the ever-useful slipcover.

The coffee table, an artifact leftover from the early-twentieth-century flirtation with Orientalia, has become part of most Americans' living room décor, regardless of the fact that it was intended to be used by people reclining on a divan or sitting on the floor (and we complain of back pains!). It has since become a useful receptacle for bibelots and coffee table books, which made their first meaningful appearance in the 1970s.

The charm of certain living rooms lies in their smallness. Tiny sitting rooms are perfect for intimate conversations; morning rooms,

Using *Kabul*, the *ikat* fabric developed
from an antique garment from
Afghanistan (see Chapter 1, p. 20),
the Boston design firm of Sandler-Dick
decorated a condo overlooking the
Charles River in Santa Fe style, with
easy furniture and Southwestern
artifacts.

where the early sun slants in, are ideal for needlework; nooks and snug-
geries that are not quite dens and not quite libraries are ideal for
reading and writing letters. All are beneficial pursuits in a more
contemplative era.

What we usually term a "contemporary" (a moveable term)
living room tends toward the post–World War II open plan, which
combines a living room with, say, a dining room, kitchen, bar, or, in
tropical climes, an indoor/outdoor sun room. "Family room" is
another term used for this type of room; its focal point is often a television set. These casual rooms are where family members gather, with
multiple activities taking place simultaneously. Does anyone remember
the "conversation pit" of the early 1950s?

This type of living room is upholstered with woven textures
rather than traditional chintzes. Curtains are not as necessary, as there
is less upholstery that will fade, and light itself may be an important
part of the design. Colors tend toward white or a subtle rainbow of
naturals: ice, vanilla, shell, clotted cream, scrubbed-and-bleached

wood, curds and whey, pearl, linen, celadon, hemp, string, slate, steel, paper-bag brown, cement, sand, bark, bronze, copper, rope, donkey brown, stone, smoke, terra-cotta, brick, heather, horn, lace, scrimshaw, fawn, wicker, cork, leather, office-machine neutrals, and anodized black accents. There's a lot to choose from! Fabrics include checks, stripes, cotton damasks, and textured wovens. Walls tend to be plain, and furniture ranges from Bauhaus and Art Deco to '50s Swedish and post-modern, with good, basic, classic upholstered pieces and the occasional antique, used almost as a piece of freestanding sculpture.

Boston designer Richard Fitz Gerald's getaway on Cape Cod reflects the casual ease of weekend houses. A mixture of Brunschwig fabrics, chosen to show as little fading as possible, including *Dysart* glazed chintz and *La Pêche* damask on the chairs and *Cavendish* sofas, circle a practical and indestructible coffee table. A coral awning keeps the midday heat from the room and the terrace that leads out to the garden.

This luxurious drawing room was designed for the 1987 Kips Bay Boys and Girls Club Showhouse by New York decorator Mario Buatta. His signature details include yellow walls, George Oakes painted cushions, needlepoint carpet, and the inevitable dog picture. The sofa and armchair are covered in Brunschwig's *Campanula* glazed chintz, and the sumptuous balloon valance is of *Trianon* striped silk.

New York designer Thomas Britt picked colors from Brunschwig's *Tyler* woven stripe for the background paintwork in this living room. Coral cushions are used as bright accents, a wonderful table with a painted base is in the background, and the whole room — and its matching dining area — is punctuated with neoclassic statuary.

This grand London drawing room in Onslow Gardens was decorated by Nicholas Haslam, who persuaded the owner, fashion designer David Sassoon, to live with a subtle palate of colors — stippled pale jade walls, natural canvas curtains, touches of *Empire* egg-yolk yellow and aubergine, and a French tapestry carpet. The combination enhances the painting of Margaret, Lady Herbert (from the studio of Van Dyke), complementing the large scale of the room. The sofa is covered in Brunschwig's *Le Zèbre* linen print, adding a chic, lighthearted touch.

Start in Paris as the fount of *le haut décor*. This room uses fabric from Braquenié, France's oldest and grandest manufacturer of fabric, tapestry, and carpets. The firm was recently acquired by Patrick Frey, who celebrated his newest asset and its glorious days in the overly elaborate Second Empire by mounting a grand showhouse of twenty rooms in three pavilions of the Bagatelle in Paris. This elegant drawing room is decorated in a classic *indienne* print that Brunschwig sells in the United States as *Kandahar*. (See Chapter 1, p. 14, and Chapter 13, p. 148, for other fabrics shown at the Bagatelle.)

Opposite: In her converted farmhouse in Old Chatham, New York, Zelina Brunschwig designed a timeless living room using a combination of formal and provincial antiques and soft upholstered pieces covered with a flowered print called *Riviera*, still a favorite of the Brunschwig collections. This room, photographed in 1969, would still be comfortable to live in today.

Living rooms can't help but reflect their regional and national differences. In France — the fount of *la décoration* — grand rooms have age, which also means architecture, and a certain formality. (See Bagatelle above, and in Chapter 1, p. 15.) Grand London flats may have a scale seldom found in American big-city apartments — high ceilings, moldings, large mantels (such as David Sassoon's, decorated by Nicholas Haslam). English country houses exude a certain look of slipcovers and Staffordshire that is much imitated by some American decorators when it's fashionable — but seldom accurately. Traversing the United States from north to south and east to west, differences are detected, though there are exceptions in every area. The East Coast still has its roots in Europe, so apartments and houses often have the mellow patina that antiques endow, exemplified in Zelina Brunschwig's 1830 farmhouse in Old Chatham. Believing that good design is forever, she designed a dateless living room for their weekend retreat way back in the 1960s, using mainly Louis XVI furniture, some refined and some provincial, interspersed with soft upholstered furnishings. Southerners maintain their family antiques, and they also use more fabric in their higher-ceilinged houses — gathered, frilled, or trimmed. Florida has even given its name to a type of tropical living room, the Florida room,

Lightness, sunniness, and casual ease make this a real Florida room. Akron, Ohio, designer Roz Travis designed it using the blue-and-white calm and simplicity of Brunschwig's *Athos*, her favorite print, combined with all-white furniture. The design of *Athos* — one of Billy Baldwin's favorites — is French, based on an eighteenth-century painted taffeta. Though the design was already a print in the Brunschwig collection, Murray Douglas was thrilled to find a piece of the original painted taffeta in the Winterthur Museum textile archives.

Opposite: Marianne Oberlin is an interior designer in Hudson, Ohio. She chose sunny yellow as the background for the living room in her 1840 house, and deliberately omitted curtains to let as much light in as possible to offset the gray winter days typical of the Midwest. She lined the alcove with a warm red to display china and objets d'art. Murray Douglas was pleased to see that the combination of the two Brunschwig prints — *Borromea*, with a yellow ground, and *Floréal* on the cushions at either end of the sofa — worked well here as it had in her own house. "I got good advice from Mrs. Douglas," says Oberlin. "She suggested the Oriental carpet on polished wood."

typified by the blue-and-white room Roz Travis designed using *Athos*. Midwesterners ache for décor with singing jewel tones or bright florals, such as Marianne Oberlin's room in the attractive Greek Revival historic district of Hudson, Ohio. Vivid colors counteract long winters, especially in those areas near the gray, shadowy clouds of the Great Lakes. The Chicago area is known for its architecture, both the traditional, European-influenced, David Adler "Great House" variety in the suburbs north of the city and the homegrown Louis Sullivan and Frank Lloyd Wright type elsewhere. The West Coast's décor owes much to David Adler's sister, Frances Elkins, and via her to the late Michael Taylor, whose work established a Californian style — off-white rooms with oversize wicker furniture and Syrie Maugham-ish bleached antiques, rough quarry-tile floors, and desert plants, all opening up to garden and swimming pool. The blinding sunniness and open air, sometimes contrasting with Hollywoodesque soft sofas in the shaded interiors, give these rooms a new and extraordinarily casual feeling, especially compared to a Parisian salon.

Los Angeles designer Dennis Wilcut
has surrounded himself in the grand-
daddy of printed fabrics, *Grand Génois*
(see Chapter 1, pp. 10–11), combining it
with ottomans covered in its filler print.
Great pictures of exotic birds, an
antique bird cage, accents of *Leopard*
velvet, and a fantasy faux-leopard carpet
complete the scene.

Isabel Fowlkes decorated her own New York apartment in dateless, traditional style using Brunschwig's *Le Lac*, a much-loved chintz developed from a chinoiserie brocaded satin made in the late eighteenth century. It was adapted into a chintz in the 1930s. Murray Douglas later found it had its own border design, so this was added to the collection. The chintz, which comes from France, is expensive because it has a very large repeat. "It stands up wonderfully," says Mrs. Fowlkes. "It's been here for ten years and only cleaned once." She added painted pillows with motifs taken from the print. One of Murray Douglas's favorite sofas — a huge one covered in this print — is in Atlanta's Swan House. (Also see *Le Lac*, used by Irvine & Fleming, on p. 95.)

Using Brunschwig's *St. Amour* beige moiré, Los Angeles decorator Janet Polizzi has designed a calm and serene living room in Aspen, Colorado.

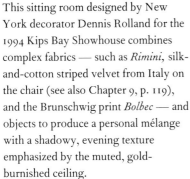

This sitting room designed by New York decorator Dennis Rolland for the 1994 Kips Bay Showhouse combines complex fabrics — such as *Rimini*, silk-and-cotton striped velvet from Italy on the chair (see also Chapter 9, p. 119), and the Brunschwig print *Bolbec* — and objects to produce a personal mélange with a shadowy, evening texture emphasized by the muted, gold-burnished ceiling.

This unpretentious living room using Brunschwig's *Adirondack* wallpaper as the background, was created by Cleveland, Ohio, designer Norma Goulder Savin for actress June Gibbons, who performs with the Guthrie Theater in Minneapolis. Classic 1950s furniture by William Stephens and Warren Platner combines with the *ikat* pattern *Kabul* on the sofa (see p. 100) and *Volnay* texture to produce a casual, heartland style.

The idiosyncratic mix of fabrics and objects in David Herchik's 1873 Washington, D.C., house includes *Montpellier* silk chenille; the *Chanson* silk cut-velvet leaf pattern in red and green; *Monaco* cut velvet; *New Fleur-de-Lys* silk; *Portsmouth* linen velvet; and *Brunschwig Ultrasuede* all in the ottoman patchwork cover. The camel-backed purple sofa is covered in mohair velvet. Herchik makes his own cushions, patchwork (such as the round ottoman), and curtains; does his own paint effects; and runs a workshop that makes curtains for other decorators.

Using a background of custom-colored beige-and-white *Treillage* wallpaper and matching borders, Boston designer Anthony Catalfano plays off muted textures and patterns in this living room for the Jewish Community Center of the North Shore showhouse in Marblehead. Brunschwig furniture includes the classic *Cavendish* sofa covered in *Monica strié* piqué and a *Wilcox* sofa and *Lowell* chairs covered with natural-colored *Trouville* linen damask. The table skirt is made of shell-and-bois de rose *Justine* silk taffeta plaid with *Gran Canale crête* trimming. The curtains are of *Ashley* cotton-and-linen print trimmed with *Valentina* cord.

Laguna Beach designer Hank Morgan decorated this California living room using *Sevenoaks*, a print based on a seventeenth-century crewel embroidery design. The original document was green wool embroidery on linen, but here the colors are reversed, with white on a blue ground.

Susan Lankenau of The Red Door in Richmond used *Les Sphinx Médaillons*, a neoclassic French cotton print, for her own living room sofa and chair. Taking a cue from the design, she created elliptical cushions and an ottoman of Chinese teapot-covered *Warwick* tapestry.

The New York team of Peter van Hattum and Harold Simmons designed this Georgetown living room in a combination of subtle patterns — paisley and subdued florals — and rich but not loud textures such as Brunschwig's cotton-and-rayon *Soligny* from Belgium on the sofa — against plain cream walls. The result is a modern take on traditional elements.

9

Dining Rooms

Opposite: For the dining room walls of the bishop's residence in Charleston, Sally Harmon Caughman selected *Les Sylphides*, based on a 1794 hand-blocked French arabesque wallpaper found in the Hathaway House in Suffield, Connecticut (a property of the Antiquarian and Landmarks Society of Hartford, Connecticut). The bishop, the Reverend David Thompson, told Ms. Caughman that he calls these wonderful winged creatures his "dancing girls"! Anchoring the design are two borders: *Wheatley*, developed from an early-nineteenth-century design, and *Entrelacs et Pirouettes*, a reproduction of a late-eighteenth- or early-nineteenth-century design, still block-printed, that simulates architectural moldings. The chandelier once belonged to the Vatican; it was discarded when candles became obsolete (it is now wired for electricity). The table and the host and guest of honor chairs were all saved from the house when it was devastated by Hurricane Hugo. The china on the table is from a custom-made service with the Diocese seal.

Right: For the chairs in Murray Douglas's house in the country, Nan Heminway picked *Mrs. Delany* seat and backs as slipcovers, using a blue-and-beige *Deauville* plaid as the classic back, tied with bows. The walls are covered in *Fondi* vinyl wallpaper.

If an apartment or house has a separate dining room, it tends to be the most formal and traditional room in the house. For inspired dinner-party givers, the dining room is significant, the place where skills converge: imaginative food, great wine, an exquisitely dressed table, efficiently served courses, and interesting guests. All too often, formal dining rooms are used only three times a year, when the family meets for special occasions.

A formal dining room should have some drama to set the scene as you enter; as the evening progresses, the interactions of the diners provide the excitement. A buffet may solve the problem of serving the dinner, but everyone's digestion is vastly improved by sitting on a hard-backed chair at a proper table.

In the past three centuries dining room walls were decorated with frescoes, tapestries, and paintings. Now wallpaper is generally used,

and it can be spectacular. It will never dominate the room. Dinner guests won't sit there staring at the walls; they will turn toward each other. Some dining rooms are hung with fabric — such as Ruben de Saavedra's dining room — or draped, both walls and ceiling, like Napoleonic tents. Trompe l'oeil drapery paper can be used to great effect. Windows can be hung with the most sumptuous of curtains, with swags and fringes and elaborate tiebacks. But perhaps all a room really needs is simple curtains of the finest quality silk taffeta, singing with color, such as Parish-Hadley's. Formality is not always needed. Fashion designer Geoffrey Beene created an imaginative, light-and-airy dining room in 1989 for his New York apartment using Brunschwig's *Les Touches*, a sophisticated fantasy leopard-spotted printed cotton, then had the walls painted in a slightly larger version of the same print. Geoffrey Bradfield's intimate dining room has big-city sophistication without being grand and formal.

During daytime this sophisticated Manhattan dining room, designed by Parish-Hadley, has a poetic, dreamlike quality. At night, filled with guests, it becomes animated. Simple *Ninon* taffeta curtains with tiny pleated edges — rosy pink on the inside, a lively jade green on the outer curtains — complement green walls embellished with pink-tinged chinoiserie-esque murals that are echoed by the carpet. The chairs are upholstered in *Eau de Nil*–colored fabric, like ballroom chairs. This is a large room where either one or two tables can be set up according to the number of guests.

The late New York designer Ruben de Saavedra designed this stylish dining room for the 1985 Kips Bay Showhouse. *Ambre* woven stripe curtains are slung around the walls, giving a smart Regency effect. This provides an opportunity to change the décor periodically, rather like slipcovering the walls.

Right: Fashion designer Geoffrey Beene created this imaginative, light-and-airy dining room for his New York apartment using *Les Touches*, a sophisticated, fantasy leopard-spotted cotton. The walls were then painted in a slightly larger version of the same pattern.

Below: Geoffrey Bradfield of Spectre-Bradfield designed this urbane and definitely nighttime dining room featuring *Rimini*, a striped velvet made in Italy.

Lighting is of paramount concern, for dining rooms tend to be nighttime spaces. Candles, sconces, chandeliers, and candelabra all help to make a dining room glamorous. An interesting screen — be it lacquered or of embossed leather or of fabric or wallpaper — can conceal the practical swing door that leads to the kitchen in most grand apartments. Sideboards and serving tables, and most of all chairs, can be antique, reproduction, or modern, but they must be stable and not difficult to maintain. Though a large table running through the center of the room is traditional, a stylish alternative is to have two or more small tables instead that are related to each other by means of matching — or deliberately contrasting — fabric. Tables can be given quilted, floor-length skirts topped by removable, unquilted cloths. Seating guests at separate, rather crowded tables induces a sort of controlled flirtatiousness and provides a way of making a party more romantic.

The owner of this amusing dining room in a house on Nantucket is mad about dogs — and everything in the house reflects this passion. Designer Barbara Morgan of One Room at a Time selected Brunschwig's *Balmoral*, with its pugs, tartan, and roses — a veritable riot of mid-Victorian motifs — as the perfect fabric.

Opposite: This dining room, which belongs to New York designer Marshall Watson, features Brunschwig's *Hollyhocks* wallpaper. The windows are dressed with undercurtains of *Tansy* lace trimmed with *Yardley* linen fringe, and a valance of *Ara* striped chintz. The table, surrounded by lacquer-and-gilt elm dining chairs, is covered in *Montabert taffetas* stripe with an underskirt of *St. Michel* damask.

Left: For casual weekend dining at his country retreat on Cape Cod, Boston designer Richard Fitz Gerald uses *Castanet* plaid cotton for a tablecloth and balloon shades. Comfortable *Caledonian* armchairs are upholstered in ink blue *Simply Suede* and crisply piped in white. On the table, a Staffordshire Benjamin Franklin surveys the scene, though he is entitled *George Washington* — English potters of the time probably didn't know the difference!

Opposite: Karin C. Weller of Cambridge, Massachusetts, created this family dining room using *Château-Landon* glazed chintz as the key. The curtains are trimmed with gold-knotted fringe and the same print is used for the tie-on seat covers. The walls are hand-painted with bold stripes. The tallboy and grandfather clock are family heirlooms, but the Italian table was found in London and given a faux porphyry top.

Left: The chairs in this Gothick dining room in New York, designed by McMillen, are upholstered in Brunschwig's *Warwick* tapestry, a fabric that imitates a *gros point* effect.

Opposite: For the dining room of her three-story Jacobean town house in Deddington, near Oxford in England, Merlin Pennink chose red *Harrow Damask* chintz for the curtains. This documentary pattern was suggested and given to Brunschwig by Keith Irvine and has proved very popular. A paisley shawl covers the table, which holds a rare collection of boot- and shoe-shaped snuffboxes for use while hunting. The parrot tulips come from Mrs. Pennink's own wonderful garden.

Toronto designer Murray Oliver designed this dining room as part of the extensive restoration of a large 1834 house called Drumsnab in Canada. Formal yet intimate, the room is unusually small for the scale of the house. Dusty rose walls of *Courtnay Strié* wallpaper are topped with a swagged red-and-green *Bosphore* border. A variety of late Regency chairs have *Linen Moiré*–striped seats. The coral curtain swags are of *Montgomery Place* wool damask, with blue-and–terra-cotta *Isabelle* fringe. The *Nicole Paisley* sheer undercurtains are trimmed with *Yardley* linen *giselle*.

The San Francisco firm Sanchez-Ruschmeyer designed this engaging dining room using a documentary-based Italian-printed chinoiserie cotton, *Marco Polo*, instead of wallpaper. This background enhances the tortoiseshell-framed looking glass and escutcheoned commode, and sets the right mood for a delectable meal.

Opposite: Any grand dinner party would be made more sumptuous by a background of *Tenture Flottante* wallpaper. This dining room is by the New York decorating firm McMillen, where Mrs. B. worked as a decorator in the 1930s. (See Ron Collier's use of the same wallpaper in Chapter 7, p. 91.)

10 🖋

Libraries

Libraries usually have a masculine tone. Perhaps this is due in part to the upper-class eighteenth- and nineteenth-century tradition of the Grand Tour, a trip taken by men to see the world and finish their education (while for the most part women stayed at home and sewed). The men returned loaded with books, folios, pictures, and antiques they had collected en route. Special rooms were put aside for the precious volumes, which had to be housed in appropriately serious splendor. The tradition has stuck, and libraries frequently are filled with dark wood paneling, leather-covered chairs, classical busts, dark green tapestries, and tartan carpeting. Pinked felt or gold-stamped leather strips on shelves are another decorative detail with roots in the past. In old private libraries, when books were far more costly, a fringe — sometimes six inches long — of fabric cut into strips was attached to each shelf to remove dust from a book, without damaging the spine, when the book was pulled out from the shelf below.

Not all libraries are masculine, serious, or sometimes even slightly pompous. Charlotte Moss in New York and Lindy Lieberman in Massachusetts have designed soft, ladylike libraries for showhouses, while Nancy Pierrepont (for her own house in New Jersey), Anne Ames in Ohio, and Eveline Peardon in Connecticut have all designed libraries for real use in unexpected but feminine colors. (See pp. 128–129, 131, and title page.)

For the 1988 Kips Bay Boys and Girls Club Decorator Showhouse, Peter van Hattum and Harold Simmons designed this traditionally masculine, wood-paneled library, enlivened by a French cotton-and-linen print called *Paradis*, seen on the curtains (trimmed with *Isabelle* fringe), on a *Bedford* chair, and on a *Piedmonte* récamier. A *Cavendish* sofa is covered with *Lambert* chenille and trimmed with *Orion grande* fringe. The pale yellow balloon shades are of *Chantelle* silk taffeta made in England, and the sofa pillows are of *Topkapi*, a silk warp print.

Left: For the armchair and ottoman in this paneled library (belonging to a scion of a prominent merchant family in Lake Forest, Illinois), decorator June G. Ashton used Brunschwig's *Pook's Hill* — named after Kipling's *Puck of Pook's Hill* — a sentimental favorite of many customers that periodically gets discontinued and then reappears in the collection. The needlepoint cushion was embroidered by June Ashton for her client — who is a good needlepointer herself. The freesias are from the greenhouse.

Above: For the 1990 Royal Oak Designer Showhouse, Charlotte Moss designed a library as the perfect place for afternoon tea. She used *Chanterac* cotton-and-linen print for the ottoman and *Katia* matelassé — an adaptation from a document at the Benaki Museum, Athens — for simple looped-back curtains trimmed with *Gabrielle* rope on tape. Wood paneling and bound books have been allowed to speak for themselves.

Right: Shaker Heights, Ohio, designer Anne Ames, knowing how much color is needed in the Midwestern light, schemed this library to be a treasure trove of gem tones. The sofa is covered in an English nineteenth-century block print, *Peony*, on linen. On it are cushions of *Kilimanjaro* and lavender *Maja* figured chintz with peony-red edging to match the red walls. A red *Regina* chair is reflected in the mirror, and Brunschwig's *Fontaine* Roman coffee table is in the foreground.

Below: For the library of her country house in New Jersey, Nancy Pierrepont selected the documentary pattern *Napoléon Trois*, emphasizing its period style with tufted upholstery and long, creamy bullion fringes. She has scattered exactly the right antique needlepoint cushions on the sofa and chairs, and anchored the room with a dark-grounded needlepoint carpet.

This warm, mellow library designed by
David Anthony Easton for the 1990
Royal Oak Designer Showhouse uses
curtains of *Vladimir* to provide a woven
texture. A tufted chair in the far corner
is covered in *Chatillon* cut velvet, while
the cushions on the sofa are a *Deepdene*
printed tapestry.

A masculine library quality is displayed
in this game room in a modern house in
Kingston, just outside London,
designed by Bill Bennette. The chairs
are covered in a cotton print called
I.O.U., adapted from a French
eighteenth-century needlework gaming
table cover. A billiard table and a bar
complete the room.

Books on shelves can be the best background ever invented. The intriguing visual variety, intellectual implication, and promise of never a dull moment give status to a room. The trick is to avoid the dreariness of institutional libraries, which is a challenge to the decorator who often prefers the eye-pleasing to the mere practicality of finding the right book.

Some rooms are called libraries in name only, with awfully pretty shelves filled with family snapshots, Lowestoft saucers, busts, classic nineteenth-century reproductions from the Archaeological Museum in Naples, Rockingham figures, plaques, mirrors, watercolors . . . and very few books. Others are full of matching bound books, an old conceit of the very rich. Books are often displayed for their beautiful old bindings; but how many volumes of Emerson does one need? Ron Collier's design for a Manhattan apartment is more a writing room or den than a library, as it contains few books but has comfortable furnishings and a practical desk for writing.

The library is a place for peace and quiet and also a classic spot for serious family talks — the ideal place to ask for the daughter's hand or to discuss money and inheritance. You need comfortable chairs arranged to induce conversation, tables and trays for drinks — aperitifs, sherry, brandy, port — and cigar boxes. Serious reading and letter writing is best done on a hard chair at a table or desk, as in the days of Jane Austen, though nowadays we are more likely to use an ergonomic office chair with a plain vanilla computer — not the easiest objects to deal with on an aesthetic level.

Ron Collier designed this room — more den than library — in a New York apartment around *Sultan of Gujarat*, a cotton-and-linen print adapted from a document in the Henry Francis du Pont Winterthur Museum. The warm and snug effect is achieved by coral walls, bamboo shades, natural wood cabinets, and generous cushions. Green glass paperweights on the desk by the window echo a green tray-table in the foreground.

Lindy Lieberman of Living Spaces in Westwood, Massachusetts, designed this library solarium for the 1993 Junior League Showhouse in Boston. The room is a sunny yet calm study in warm neutrals, from cream to brown. The walls are papered with a beige version of *Talavera*, a pattern based on an original found by Mrs. Douglas in a Hudson River house. (See Chapter 6, p. 74.) The pattern has also been used on cloth, as on the cotton-and-linen print seen here, and as a silk warp print.

Left: The New York interior design firm McMillen decorated this traditional library using *Fleurs Indiennes* cotton-and-linen border print. *Kilimanjaro* tapestry, patterned in leopard spots, is used on a chair in the foreground; *Oatlands,* a *gros point* fabric, is on a cushion. The *Portsmouth* linen velvet on the sofa is a useful fabric because it comes in many different colors.

Opposite: This library decorated by Mark Hampton for the 1980 Kips Bay Showhouse is handsome in its simplicity. The architectural bones of the room already existed. The walls were dark, with the moldings and mantle painted white. White *New Richmond Dimity,* with its characteristic subtle woven stripe, is used on all the upholstered pieces, including the plump, down-filled cushions edged with barely discernible pleated edges. The high quality of the antique furnishings and paintings is played down by a natural sisal wall-to-wall carpet. Shelves full of obviously much-read books provide the lifelike background.

Left: London designer Morrow Reis combined shades of brown, rust, and beige in this library–living room in everything from the geometric carpet to the bold painting of a woman in a rusty red jerkin, the brown ribbon–patterned blinds, the books, a paisley shawl, Brunschwig's paisley print *Chatham,* and the tabby cat. The effect is serene and composed.

II 🖋

Kitchens

Of all the rooms in a house, the kitchen is the one most likely to be "space designed" but not "decorated." Many turn over the organization of their kitchen to specialists in time and motion studies. One woman insisted that her contractor build a plywood dummy of her kitchen work station so she could make sure that the final, expensive installation would be perfect. Others insist on cupboards that open at the push of an electronic button, central vacuum systems, ceiling rollers for tablecloths so they never show a wrinkle, madly desirable Garland stoves, or refrigerators bigger than armoires.

Kitchens are workrooms — they are always being remodeled and updated. It is often a costly procedure, because owners may insist on the newest appliances surrounded by built-in granite counters. Because these appliances take up room, there is little space — or money — left for much more than a border of wallpaper. Diana Walker of Morristown, New Jersey, solved this problem by papering the appliances! Curtains tend to be small, often sheer, and included only for privacy or to hide an ungainly view (as is so often the case in New York apartments where the kitchen looks out onto a fire escape and the well of an adjacent building). There are, however, many patterns of fabric and wallpaper that are amusing, novel, or just plain good-looking in a kitchen. Classic checks and stripes, simple geometrics, florals, and provincial prints are suitable. The trick is to use designs that are not too opulent, though all rules can be broken in the right hands — there is

Morristown, New Jersey, designer Diana Walker found a way to use wallpaper in her kitchen by papering not only the walls, but also the cupboards, drawers, and appliances too. Using Brunschwig's *Jardinière*, crisp white paint, white and patterned tiles inside the stove area, curved terra-cotta roof tiles on the stove hood, terra-cotta tiles on the floor, a battery of copper saucepans, and lots of greenery, she created a cheerful, welcoming yet practical space.

Using modern textures — including Brunschwig's *Lido* — and neutral colors, New York designer Tom O'Toole created this uncluttered, contemporary living room–kitchen on the lower level of the 1981 Kips Bay Boys and Girls Club Showhouse, forecasting a more tailored look of the future.

Opposite: Marcia Doering, head of the Brunschwig & Fils showroom in Beachwood, Ohio, used *Hare and Hound* wallpaper border and sidewall in her own kitchen. The pattern is printed on vinyl, making it very practical. It was derived from crewel bed hangings in the Henry Francis du Pont Winterthur Museum, and it works well with the red-painted cupboards and refrigerator. On the floor, not shown, Ms. Doering painted a variation of Brunschwig's *Crossgrain*, with a hare and a hound in each corner.

one glamorous kitchen in New York that is hung with one of the most expensive arcaded wallpapers in the world! Brunschwig & Fils can put special finishes on wallpapers or print them on vinyl, and put a Teflon finish on fabrics to make them dirt- and stain-resistant, which is practical in a kitchen.

Many people spend a great deal of time in their kitchen or a nearby breakfast room. If it is large, with a country table, the kitchen often becomes a living room where meals are prepared and eaten. The days when the cook kept everyone out of the kitchen are, for most, in the past. Everyone, including the man of the house, has become interested in the preparation of food. Today's casual way of living allows our friends to share a cup of tea at the kitchen table, help prepare an elaborate dinner, or make sandwiches for a picnic. Family members and acquaintances are welcome in what was once almost forbidden territory. For this reason, kitchens need to be congenial and attractive, whether they are sleek and high-tech or cozy and old-fashioned — or somewhere in between.

When Sybil Connolly and Murray Douglas conceived the decoration for this kitchen in the Cottage Orné in Ireland (see Chapter 6, p. 78), for wallpaper and border they picked *Cahir* — pronounced "care," the Irish way — a pattern named after the town of Cahir in Tipperary. Mrs. Douglas's watercolor shows a wonderfully evocative country kitchen, complete with a classic mixing bowl, a bunch of carrots, and a tea towel on a scrubbed wood table; a Shaker rocking chair (yes, these were imported from America); a barrel of potatoes; blue-and-white-checked squabs on the kitchen chairs; a mantlepiece with dish and candles; a dresser with blue-and-white pottery; a salt box; and a Gothick window looking out over the Irish scene.

Designer Barbara Southerland of Greenville, North Carolina, and New York created this unusual butler's pantry in use as a flower-arranging room, for the 1990 Royal Oak Showhouse. Dominating the room is Brunschwig's midnight blue–ground colorway of the pattern *Mafalda*. (A very different use of *Mafalda* can be seen in Chapter 14, p. 164.)

12 🖎

Bathrooms & Powder Rooms

New York decorator Stephen Stempler used *Les Scapins* wallpaper in this glamorous dressing room designed for the 1992 Kips Bay Showhouse. The wallpaper was developed from *singeries* — dressed-up monkey decorations on a harpsichord in the château at Thoiry. (See Chapter 6, p. 76.) With all the mirrors in this photograph, see if you can find the camera!

Private bathrooms as we now know them are recent additions to the domestic interior. In the Far East and ancient Rome people bathed communally as a social event. In the eighteenth century bathrooms were a novelty, though water closets existed in the grander English houses. Benjamin Franklin invented a shoe-shaped sitz bath and cautiously recommended its use, but the relationship between cleanliness and health was not generally known until the nineteenth century. As with kitchens, bathrooms nowadays are much used and full of essential gadgets — medicine cabinets, scales, hair dryers, showers, washbasins, toothbrush racks, soap dishes, bidets, towel racks, electric shavers, toilet paper holders, mirrors and magnifying mirrors — and of course the essential privy, which has always been given euphemistic names, from lavatory, loo, or ladies or "gents" cloakroom in England to toilet or "john" in America. Bathrooms are frequently renovated, and their engineering is continually upgraded. Some old bathrooms — and by old we mean sixty to a hundred years old — have a quaint kind of charm that is now much sought-after, with claw-foot tubs, wide-edged washbasins, and vintage bathroom fixtures. But those who want a cozy, old-fashioned look usually also insist on having the latest plumbing.

Fashions come and go in bathroom decoration as they do for all rooms. In the 1960s off-beat, colored fixtures were à la mode — but black bathrooms are especially difficult to keep clean because every water spot shows. Patrick Willoughby, an English designer in Lincolnshire, worked existing orange fixtures to his clients' advantage using *Shimo* wallpaper (see Chapter 6, p. 75). In the energy-reckless 1980s, whirlpools, saunas, and mammoth sunken bathtubs were fashionable. Couples now say that separate washbasins are an excellent idea, and separate bathrooms are in greater demand than separate bedrooms. Bathrooms and dressing rooms are increasingly used for

Above: In this high-style powder room, a nineteenth-century English bamboo cabinet with black-and-gold chinoiserie panels has been fitted up with modern plumbing and set against a background of *Vintage Royal* wallpaper, inspired by Brighton Pavilion (from the Royal Pavilion collection). (See Chapter 6, pp. 73–74.)

Above, right: For this 1989 Designer Showhouse in Washington, D.C., Marie Johnston designed a crisp and practical bathroom using red-colorway *Cahir* wallpaper, first introduced in the Cottage Orné collection. (For another use of *Cahir* see Chapter 11, p. 138.)

private sybaritic indulgence — to exercise, pamper the body, read in the tub — whether the room is lush and voluptuous or simple and spartan.

The term "powder room" is euphemistic, dating to earlier in the twentieth century when women did actually powder their noses. "It was a déclassé term I was encouraged not to use," says Murray Douglas. "Saying 'cloakroom' was fine, even if there were no cloaks." However, these small, downstairs washrooms give the designer a chance to use fantastic, novel, dramatic, sophisticated, or very extravagant paper. Though the space may be small — such as the powder room designed by Richard Neas for a New York family, using *Vintage Royal* wallpaper — they can be tiny jewel boxes of rooms, and there is a wealth of exotic bathroom fixtures available as well as antique pieces that can be adapted to modern plumbing.

Select practical furniture for any bathroom. Bamboo, vintage Lloyd Loom chairs, casual antiques, and shells add a pleasing touch. Include nothing that can be damaged by water. Bear in mind that steamy showers tend to ease wallpaper off walls; sitting in a bathtub is less destructive. One way to bring decoration into a bathroom is to frame a mirror with a wallpaper border rather than to paper the whole

For a house — once a library — on the eastern end of Long Island, New York, interior designer Carl D'Aquino and architect Paul Laird concocted this sleek master bathroom with tongue-in-chic neo-Victoriana. Specially designed cabinet work includes a spindly legged, exaggeratedly rounded washbasin. D'Aquino added a curvacious uphol-stered *St. Honoré* chair covered in *New Cholet Plaid*, with the addition of heavy bullion *Traviata* fringe making an allu-sion to — but gently mocking — the High Victorian style.

wall. Murray Douglas used *Convolvulus* border on only the mirror in her country bathroom. Others like an elaborate fabric shower curtain with a plastic liner inside to protect it, and washbasins with skirts attached by Velcro to hide the plumbing.

Lighting is important. Always place a light over the toilet, and make sure that mirrors and lights are flattering. Slipper chairs can be slipcovered in terry toweling. Towels can be customized by adding borders of printed fabric. Wallpapers can be amusing, such as *Scapins*'s dressed-up monkeys, used in Stephen Stempler's mirrored dressing room (p. 140), or the high hedge of *La Haie* panel, which has an image that is thick enough to give a feeling of privacy yet is daring because of the feeling of being outdoors. (See Chapter 13, p. 155.)

Left: For a house in Kingston, outside London, Bill Bennette chose *Chinese Blossoms* for a bedroom and its private, luxurious bathroom. In this pale pink coloring, the pattern was one of Billy Baldwin's favorites.

Opposite: This glamorous California bathroom with paneled wood walls and a Jacuzzi was designed by Lynn Deal of Newport Beach, who chose *Calceolaria* cotton-and-linen print from England as a key fabric. The print design shows colorful flowers with a blue ribbon on a white ground. Knowledgeable gardeners will look for the little purse-shaped flowers.

13 🖋

Bedrooms & Dressing Tables

As with living rooms, bedrooms often require the use of a lot of fabric. They are also likely to include wallpaper in their decoration. As in the eighteenth-century painting by Boucher at the very beginning of this book, fabric is sometimes used traditionally, en suite, for bed, walls, and window curtains.

Grand bedrooms demand lavish amounts of fabric to dress canopy beds. Sometimes these are lined with a contrasting fabric and trimmed with yet another fabric or edged with passementerie. Often the same fabric is used on a quilted coverlet or to upholster chairs or dressing-table stools, and it may also be used for the window curtains.

One such bedroom that makes sumptuous use of fabric was seen in a photograph taken at the Bagatelle in Paris in an extravagant, opulent, Second Empire dream for a little princess (see p. 148). The room contained panels, trimmings, and borders of an Indo-Persian design, *Les Arcades*, and complex passementerie. It is a perfect exercise in the art of the showhouse, and it echoes France's preoccupation with the restoration of state bedrooms of the great châteaux.

Also glamorous, but a real room for a real person, is Ann Gray's Chicago bedroom dressed in the *chiné* print *Gloire*, a silk so perfectly woven that it is hard to believe it is a warp-dyed fabric. Nancy Pierrepont's *Marianthi* bedroom, designed for one of New York's busiest and best-loved philanthropists, has superb flair and shows a sure

Ann Gray's glamorous Chicago bedroom uses the *chiné* print *Gloire*, a skillfully woven, warp-printed silk from France showing flowers on a cream ground. The beauty of the cloth is that it is light and airy like a taffeta, yet is the same on both sides, unlike other prints. (See Chapter 1, p. 21.) When Ann Gray ordered this fabric, she was told there would be a three-year wait for delivery because the fabric takes so long to produce. She was thrilled when it arrived after only nineteen months.

This grand bedroom in France, shown at the Bagatelle exhibition, was supposedly designed for a child — a very grand child. It contains a series of Braquenié fabrics based on classic Indo-Persian designs: an arcaded columned panel; the columns as continuous stripes; an all-over of birds and carnations; a formal flowered stripe; and a wide stripe of *médaillons*, *bouquets*, and *sirènes;* each available separately, making eight different designs in *Les Arcades* series. The bed — a *lit à la Polonaise* — is a wonderful fantasy, with exuberant curtains caught back by elaborate tasseled *embrasses* (tiebacks), and a bedspread scalloped and hung with complex passementerie.

This very feminine bedroom, recently designed by Nancy Pierrepont for one of Manhattan's liveliest nonagenarians, is decorated in *Marianthi,* a glazed chintz with a pink ground that is named after its designer at Brunschwig, Marianthi Raptis. The walls, curtains and valances, and bed hangings are all of the same flowered print, but because they have been handled with skill and restraint, the effect is not overpowering. In fact, it is one of the prettiest bedrooms in New York.

In decorating this guest room in Albert and Murray Douglas's house in the country, Nan Heminway followed the en suite convention of using the same toile fabric for the curtains and wall coverings. Picking the lively red-on-yellow colorway of *West Indies* toile — a documentary adaptation from Historic Cherry Hill in Albany, New York — simple country furniture, and a family heirloom embroidered coverlet, the room imparts easy, welcoming comfort. The collection of needlepoint pictures was begun by Mrs. B.

Washington, D.C., designer David Herchik reveals his quirky, unconventional point of view with his own master bedroom, where the fabrics are textured, patterned, dusky, and antiqued in appearance. The window curtains — edged with *Frange Torse*, blinds, and bed hangings — are of custom-colored *Drummond* printed on sateen. The bed pillows, a fluke discovery from Italy, exactly match the lining of the golden apricot bed curtains, which are of *Lenore* faille taffeta edged with antique braid. The bedspread fabric is *Douchka* woven tapestry, the chair is covered in *Vladimir* woven texture, and a tapestry-covered cushion has a green metallic fringe from Brunschwig. The lamp shade on Brunschwig's black tole square urn lamp is *Quadrillage* plaid taffeta with fan edging. The walls and ceiling are stenciled and hand-painted by David Herchik.

hand in the way the bed hangings and the valances are draped — as if they just happened — showing the printed fabric to advantage (see opposite, middle).

Bedrooms are often fantasy rooms with a strikingly personal point of view, such as David Herchik's richly patterned yet oddly unconventional master bedroom (above).

Simpler bedrooms, usually without grand bed canopies, are often more contemporary in feeling. Toile is a classic bedroom fabric, such as the unusual yellow-ground *West Indies* toile seen in Murray Douglas's country house or *Bromley Hall* toile found in a Claude Guidi–designed London flat.

Dressing tables can be wonderfully romantic, with great cream puffs of *point d'esprit*, like the one in Jeannie McKeogh's bedroom in New Orleans (see p. 150).

Children's bedrooms require yet another quality, from babies' nurseries (such as Marie Johnston's showhouse bedroom for twins on p. 150) and sweet little girls' rooms to rooms with bunk beds, which all children at some stage in their lives find very exciting. Most of us can remember with nostalgia the rooms we slept in as children, even though they may have been cramped, rumpled, or tucked awkwardly under the

eaves. Boys' rooms tend to be tough, using rugged fabrics with bold checks and stripes or prints with motifs such as duck decoys. (Nancy Eddy's study-bedroom for a youth, however, shows a sophisticated use of *La Portugaise* and *English Leopard*, on p. 153.)

Country bedrooms have a unique charm, especially when they are understated with bare-bones furniture, rustic beams, a fan and skylight, sheer curtains, or a glass door leading into the countryside, as in the Patricia Falkenberg–designed bedroom in Pound Ridge (see p. 153).

The tropical bedroom depends on cross-breezes from windows opening onto the sea, with muslin curtains fluttering and fans whirring. Simple furnishings of local mahogany, wicker, and rattan; mirrors framed in shells; cool uncarpeted floors; and cotton fabrics in patterns that take maximum wear and minimum care enhance the tropical feeling.

Marie Johnston designed this show-house bedroom for young twins — hence, there's two of everything! The *Carolina* print was inspired by embroidered mull curtains found at the Historic Charleston Foundation in Charleston, South Carolina. *Peaweed* and *Pajama* stripe have been used on the bed canopies. The trellis and cloud wallpaper is *Capistrano*.

Above, left: Swathed in antique *point d'esprit* found in a New Orleans French Quarter shop, this dressing table, decked with antique scent bottles, stands against red-on-cream *Bosphore Semis* wallpaper. The lamp shade is trimmed with *Katrina* beaded fringe. This bedroom vignette is by New Orleans designer Jeannie McKeogh, who also specializes in painting furniture and finials. Here a 1920s vanity stool has been decorated to enhance the *Annick* printed brocade with which it is upholstered.

Wendy Reynolds of Cheever House Designs in Boston designed this serene bedroom. The swag-and-jabot curtains feature *Lady Margaret* glazed chintz, which is also used (unseen) for bed hangings and dust ruffles. *Heather* dotted swiss makes the half curtains; *Ivy Madras* lace is used as a dressing table skirt. Soft yellow glazed walls set off the English porcelains.

The Los Angeles firm Brown-Buckley created this guest room for a fashion designer, swathing it in yards of *Chinese Leopard* toile — an example of chic opulence. This is the client's favorite fabric (who has used it in different colorways also for a house in the desert) as well as being one of Brunschwig's most popular designs.

For this bedroom in the Rogers Memorial Southampton Showhouse, the late New York designer Robert Metzger and his associate Michael Christiano chose a favorite design, Brunschwig's *Ménars*, for a bordered panel to cover the uneven walls, gathering it onto rods under a buckram-stiffened valance. The massive bed was placed in the center, and the border design inspired the painted rug. (For *Ménars* in the Wrightsman's house in Palm Beach, see Chapter 1, p. 13.)

Opposite: This Pound Ridge bedroom with doors opening up to the woods was designed by Patricia Falkenberg of Scarsdale, New York. Its bare beams, built-in bedside shelves, and drawered wood-frame bed are a perfect foil for *Gstaad* cotton, printed in Switzerland, on the bed and chaise and *Egan Bey* printed on a heavy, ribbed fabric from Spain — on the large bed cushion and the small bench.

Claude Guidi, who has an office in New York, designed this Belgravia flat for Americans living in London. "They think of it as being very English!" he says. Perhaps this is because of the *Bromley Hall* toile on the chair. (See Chapter 1, p. 16, for the original document.) The general effect is purely American, however — clean and contemporary with *Chalais* cotton-and-linen plaid on the walls.

Nancy Eddy of Dedham, Massachusetts, designed this bedroom for the Junior League Decorators' Showhouse in Needham, Massachusetts. It features *La Portugaise* in a brown stripe and a comforter of *English Leopard*, a cotton print developed from a document at the Winterthur Museum. Judging from the straw boater on the bedpost, the Yale insignia on the jacket, and the silver mug of pencils and the book about Wall Street on the desk, the room is wittily intended for an almost-grownup boy!

Right: New York designers Carl D'Aquino and Geordi Humphreys decorated this master bedroom in a Pennsylvania farmhouse, assembling an inlaid sleigh bed, carved gilt mirror, lace curtains, and marvelous 1750 William Vile dressing commode. To allow the owners to hide away from the world in privacy, they chose *La Haie* (The Hedge) wallpaper, which adds a witty and novel touch.

Opposite: Unusual but feminine colors decorate this bedroom designed by Clare Fraser for the 1993 Kips Bay Designer Showhouse. The style is right for the 1990s in its use of restrained, unembellished woven fabrics. The pale lime green and plain white bed hangings are of *Watteau* silk taffeta, an Indian silk that comes in over thirty colorways. The room is ladylike in the simplicity of its fabrics, the soft sheen of its *Fujita* fringe — a crystal passementerie — and its high-quality furniture.

Right: The wallpaper in this bedroom created by McMillen is Brunschwig's *Chinoiserie*, an adaptation of a French eighteenth-century wallpaper made for the Museum of Early Southern Decorative Arts in Old Salem, North Carolina.

Opposite: This view from the bed in Nancy Pierrepont's country house shows a delicate use of Brunschwig's *Locklin Plantation* glazed chintz, an adaptation from a Brunschwig archival wallpaper that was made for the historic museum house Liberty Hall in Kenansville, North Carolina. Well-placed pictures, personal and family memorabilia on the mantel, and peonies fresh-picked from the garden complete the scene.

M B DOUGLAS '94

Guadeloupe glazed chintz is a perfect print for a West Indies setting, shown here in Murray Douglas's watercolor of a bedroom in her St. Croix house. The bedspread is made of a simple pink-and-white colorway of *Hamilton Dimity*.

The four-poster bed reproduced from the nearby Whim Plantation is swathed in *Moustiquaire* sheer cotton.

For her house in St. Croix, Murray
Douglas selected *Antigua* check, from
the En Vacances collection, to create a
relaxed, tropical bedroom that can catch
the cross-breezes and the reflected aqua-
marine sparkle of the Caribbean.

14 ❦

Indoor / Outdoor Rooms

In a continent like North America that has such a varied climate, there are times of the year when northerners and "snow birds" ache for the sun. Thus midwesterners create solariums to catch every ray during winter. Florida rooms open out onto beaches or lush tropical greenery. California rooms are only a sliding glass door away from the swimming pool or a path leading down to the Pacific. In Charleston, South Carolina, single and double houses evolved many-tiered piazzas to catch every available breeze during the long humid summers. On Barbados and Mustique in the West Indies, Oliver Messel designed houses like stage settings, with side wings from which to make entrances and exits and pavilions leading to the warm Caribbean.

In England, where one meets uncertain weather more often than not, glass-roofed and plant-lined conservatories are used as sun rooms. Gazebos are given to flights of fancy, such as the one at Merlin Pennink's Jacobean house near Oxford (see p. 160). France developed the orangerie to shelter exotic trees during the winter months. And all around the Mediterranean, from Saint-Tropez to Taormina, life is lived on porches, loggias, and verandas.

These indoor / outdoor rooms can run the gamut from the utter simplicity of a thatched roof on stilts to the grandeur of a Palm Beach salon. As we become more worldly, sun rooms become more decorated. If fabric is used, its color must be chosen to stand up to the sun and to reflect the light, not absorb it. Many Brunschwig domestic fabrics come with a Teflon finish, and the imported ones can be Teflon

This rustic garden room was conceived by Barbara Ostrom of Mahwah, New Jersey and New York for the 1991 Greenwich Showhouse. Linen and cotton *Filoli* tapestry was used for the curtains with *Ramsey* plaid slipcovers with self ties covering the dining chairs.

treated on request. Teflon is the latest and best finish available to help stave off moisture, oil stains, and dirt; but nothing has yet been invented to prevent fabric from fading, unless the dye is deeply embedded in vinyl fiber.

California artist John Botz designs many fabrics for Brunschwig & Fils. This relationship developed when Murray Douglas became intrigued by his paintings, which often depict bright, clear, and sunny fabrics he himself had designed. Commissioned to work on the En Vacances collection, he produced a range of designs in the tradition of Suzanne Fontan, a talented French print designer of the '30s and '40s. John Botz designs can be seen in the Jane Rosemond–designed Pennsylvania pool house (opposite) and Julie Perin Bird's showhouse room (see Chapter 6, p. 86).

Sun rooms aim at simplicity — floors that feel good to bare feet; big cushions to flop back into; wicker, cane, and bamboo; metal and plastic furniture; and blinds rather than draperies, to adjust to the sun. Prints should be cool — ferns, ivies, florals, palms. And, ideally, these rooms should feel as if you could simply hose them down.

Merlin Pennink, a talented gardener, flower arranger, decorator, and antique dealer, built this gazebo in memory of her mother. It is in the walled garden of her Jacobean town house in Deddington, near Oxford. Mrs. Pennink chose the flower-covered French glazed chintz *Ariana* to make the cushions for this gazebo and also for the upholstery in her nearby conservatory.

Murray Douglas was so intrigued by Manhattan architect Lee Harris Pomeroy's copper-domed belle epoque tower gazebo that she painted a watercolor of it. Pomeroy converted it into a library for his wife, a classics scholar, using *Chrysso* damask as upholstery for the single armchair under the dome and for the chaise on the outdoor deck. *Chrysso* is an adaptation in linen and cotton of a document from the Benaki Museum in Athens, Greece. Pomeroy's circular library is lined with maple bookshelves on two levels, connected by a winding metal-plated stair.

Before the swimming pool was installed, this building was used as kennels for boarding dogs. Transformed into a pool house, it was decorated by Jane Rosemond of Sugartown Interiors, in Haverford, Pennsylvania, using *San Marino* and *Pasadena*, both cotton-and-linen prints with a Teflon finish. Designed by John Botz, these patterns come from Brunschwig's En Vacances collection. (See Julie Perin Bird's living room, Chapter 6, p. 86; and Ralph Harvard's sun room, p. 162.)

In this watercolor, Murray Douglas shows a tropical use of *Canton*, a John Botz cotton print of swirling Chinese fish, on her porch/dining room in St. Croix. A glimpse of the same pattern from the En Vacances collection can be seen in Julie Perin Bird's showhouse room (Chapter 6, p. 86).

For the 1993 Rogers Memorial Library showhouse in Southampton, Ralph Harvard of R. Brooke designed this large sun room. The printed cotton-and-linen check on the sofa is called *Antigua*. The *Cabana* stripe has a Teflon finish; a coordinating wallpaper is available. The white *Katia* cotton matelassé shown here is an adapted documentary from the Benaki Museum in Athens, Greece. The painting is by Graham Nickson.

For this chair, shown at a picnic by a lake on Cape Cod, Richard Fitz Gerald used *St. Gallen*, a Swiss cotton print depicting hot-air balloons. Echoing the ballooning motif is the rug on the grass. Surveying the scene are two visiting Canada geese.

In this breakfast room/sun room, Mary Southworth of Southworth Interiors in Lake Forest, Illinois, chose *Angela* glazed chintz from England for the curtains; a pretty French rose-and-white woven-cotton design of flowers set in diamonds, called *Blanzac*, for the upholstery; and green-and-white *Ramsey* plaid on the chairs, echoing the green tile floor and the collection of majolica.

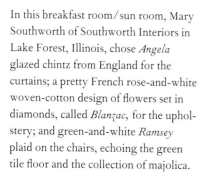

Seen here in midwinter as a *jardin d'hiver*, Robert L. Hunker's solarium/ living room in Peninsula, Ohio, was converted from a barn. The room radiates sophistication. His collection of Chinese figures and jade complements the signed Empire furniture, upholstered with neoclassic *Lannes Empire* damask seats and backs. These are sold by the set and come in white, red, gold, and green; they are woven in France. The original, worn-out, gold-colored damask that was on the chairs when Mr. Hunker acquired them is now preserved for posterity; one piece went to Winterthur and another has been framed and hung on the wall.

This breakfast room in Kingston, near London, was designed by Bill Bennette. He chose *Moorea* glazed chintz as the theme print. The height of luxury in England is an indoor swimming pool, which can be seen through the sliding door.

Nan Heminway suggested a documentary cotton print from France, *Les Fastes Persans*, for this comfortable sun porch/ winter solarium in Murray and Albert Douglas's country house. The slate floor makes it a practical room for keeping plants. Cushions are of *Potomac* linen check from Belgium, a fabric that comes in blue as well as red, and "hasn't faded yet," says Murray.

Left: For this solarium in a Lake Forest house, June G. Ashton of Chicago used *Mafalda* cotton print with a cream ground. The design of flowers and Chinese jars, printed in Italy, echoes the Chinese tobacco jar behind the nine-teenth-century French bird cage and the hibiscus from the greenhouse. Skipper, the thirty-year-old family parrot, looks on. (*Mafalda* in a dark ground is shown in Chapter 11, p. 139.)

Left: Fenwick Cottage glazed chintz — a documentary pattern based on an orig-inal watercolor, circa 1840, found in an English archive — is designed in the spirit of the Cottage Orné collection but was presented a year later. New Orleans designer Jeannie McKeogh used this print for the seat on this hand-carved chair; the rest of the chair is painted to match.

Opposite: The usually temperate North-west coastal climate — not unlike England's — is great for gardeners. Catching the sun makes sense here. Seattle's Bradley Huson has captured it using the white ground and large repeat of an *Anémones* cotton print from France, played against *Priscilla* plaid cotton taffeta, which gives the room a young, vital, relaxed point of view.

15 🙝

Public & Professional Spaces

Opposite: Using one of Brunschwig's most popular designs, *Westbury Bouquet,* Yves Taralon designed the Hediard restaurant in Paris with charm to match its good food. The design comes on glazed chintz or on linen-and-cotton cloth, in eight colorways, and is printed in Switzerland. It is an adaptation from a 1920s block print found at Old Westbury Gardens in Old Westbury, New York. Companion fabrics include *English Ivy* glazed chintz and the latest addition, *Westbury Roses.*

Right: Brunschwig's Ross Francis happened to be staying at the ANA Hotel, formerly the New Westin Hotel, in Washington, D.C., when she recognized the *Lilliana* tapestry on the sofas in the lobby. The fabric, made in France, is not a contract design but came from the regular Brunschwig collection. *Lilliana* is an adaptation from a needlework document with a *gros point* quality that was found at the Winterthur Museum in Delaware. It is available in black and green, as seen here, or red and green. The interior is designed by Sarah Tomerlin Lee, of New York.

"Hospitality" is the general trade term for the design of hotels, motels, inns, clubs, restaurants, and other spaces where the public is entertained. "Contract work" is a term mostly used for offices and other public or professional areas. "Health care" design is for hospitals, nursing homes, and doctors' offices. In addition to making special products for all these spaces, Brunschwig has also been involved in providing products for trains and yachts — even the Boston water shuttle.

Aided by shelter magazines, interior design has become a topic of general conversation. Contractors and hotel owners, hospital managers, and doctors are all becoming educated to the nuances, possibilities, and subliminal benefits of being in pleasant surroundings.

Public spaces must be cheerful but not too personal, comfortable and nonconfrontational, and luxurious but practical. Because of the public's growing sophistication, hotels now use classic prints such as *Verrières* and *Westbury Bouquet,* which in some cases are less expensive

For the curtains of this corner office at J. O. Patterson in Atlanta, Georgia, designer Ginny Magher selected *Hameau* taffeta plaid in a blue colorway. Made in Italy of bemberg and viscose, the curtains are trimmed with *Traviata* marabout fringe. The midnight blue wool-texture *Winthrop*, on the sofa, is reversible, mothproofed, and made in England. It comes in five colorways. *Monaco* linen-and-cotton cut velvet is used for the armchairs. Antique needlepoint cushions help individualize the room.

Using a custom coloring of *Navajo* cotton print stripe, Danielle Jo Garr designed this room in the pediatrics ward of the United Western Medical Center in Santa Ana, California. Even the intensive care unit of the pediatrics ward is decorated in the same bright stripe — an unusual choice, but it is psychologically beneficial for the children to know that they are not in an isolated area but are part of the same ward.

The antebellum John Rutledge House Inn in Charleston, South Carolina, was built in 1763 by John Rutledge, a delegate to the Constitutional Convention and brother to a signer of the Declaration of Independence. A loving restoration has revealed beautiful details of the house's eighteenth- and nineteenth-century architecture, with its hand-carved Italian marble fireplaces, original plaster moldings, inlaid floors, and graceful ironwork displaying Charleston's palmetto and Federal eagle motifs. Wine and sherry are served in this ballroom, where patriots, statesmen, and presidents have met. Much of the history of South Carolina and of the United States can be traced to meetings that took place here and in the library on the second floor. *Osborn* arcaded panels paper the walls, and a broad band of deep purple frames the top below the crown molding. *Osborn* is based on an American document from the Society for the Preservation of New England Antiquities (SPNEA), and originally was a flocked wallpaper.

ordered in hospitality quantities. Architects who specialize in hospitality, health care, and contract work are discovering that they need a decorator's touch to soften and humanize a public area and avoid a sterile effect. Hotels can be grand or simple, but they must have a warm, inviting feeling.

It is well known that pleasant offices produce more work. (See Ginny Magher's design for the J. O. Patterson corner office in Atlanta. Children feel more relaxed in an attractive hospital room such as Danielle Jo Garr's room for a pediatric wing in Santa Ana. A private club can be more personal than a hotel. Members of a traditionally decorated country club — such as the New Albany Country Club in Ohio, decorated by Irvine & Fleming — can feel as if they are at home (pp. 174–175). So can the faculty in the Harvard Faculty Club, decorated by Karin Weller (p. 171). Harvard has also been Brunschwigized abroad. The celebrated house near Florence where Bernard Berenson held forth, I Tatti, with its cascade of ravishing gardens, was bequeathed to Harvard. Walter Kaiser, who is in charge, selected and commissioned fabrics that are in keeping with the house's august reputation.

This watercolor by Murray Douglas shows the French library in I Tatti, outside Florence, Italy. The villa, which started as a sixteenth-century farmhouse, belonged to American art historian Bernard Berenson, who endowed it to Harvard. Since 1961 it has been known as Harvard University's Center for Italian Renaissance Studies. When it was refurbished, Harvard's Walter Kaiser selected Brunschwig fabrics.

The red curtains in this room are *I Tatti* damask. The damask, named for the villa, was inspired by a seventeenth-century document that was hung behind a painting, a familiar decorating detail in such houses (see also the green textile behind the Madonna and Child painting). Through the window is a glimpse of the Tuscan landscape and the wonderful gardens for which I Tatti is famed.

Brunschwig's *Gallier Diamond* wall-paper as shown here is named after New Orleans's Gallier House in the French Quarter. Asked to find a suitable wall-paper for the house's restoration, Brunschwig discovered this Directoire documentary pattern in its archives. It was not actually used in the house, because it was determined that its design of geometric diamonds is from an earlier period than the mid-nineteenth-century house.

This room in the Harvard Faculty Club, designed by Karin Weller, is the private dining room of the college president. She also decorated the members' dining room, and is gradually redoing much of the club.

Left: This cocktail lounge — complete with overstuffed chairs and a baby grand — on the American-European Express train that operated between Washington, D.C., and Chicago, was designed by Melissa Spann and Sally Malloy of Bay Point Interiors using Brunschwig fabrics from all over the world. In the foreground, a loveseat is covered in *Kimono*, a patterned fabric from Italy; *La Pêche* wool damask, made in England, covers the foreground chairs; *Ceruse* woven-cotton texture from France covers those farther back; and *Metropolis* embossed *Jockey* leather upholsters the walls.

Below: Dennis Rolland designed this gazebo, *The Maharajah's Tea Party*, to be auctioned for the benefit of the Cooper-Hewitt Museum. He used vividly colored Brunschwig taffetas, *Boiserie* wood mold fringe, and orange ostrich feathers. The gazebo can be easily taken apart and reassembled. All the furniture and a vintage tea set were included. Photographed on a cold, windy day in a courtyard in Queens, New York, outside his upholstery workroom, the effect — luxury against decay — is as surrealistic as a Cocteau movie.

Brunschwig fabrics have also been seen in movies, including Merchant and Ivory's *Mr. and Mrs. Bridge*, where the effect of genteel-but-shabby old money was accurate, and *Bonfire of the Vanities*, where production designer Richard Sylbert used *Treillage* wallpaper and *Sarah Jane* glazed-chintz curtains to convey the needed society swank. In the movie *Wolf*, starring Jack Nicholson, *Forêt Foliage* wallpaper was glimpsed in a hotel room. (See Chapter 7, p. 93.) Brunschwig fabrics have also been seen on television, in *The Thorn Birds* among many other programs. New Jersey designer Diana Walker selected Brunschwig fabrics for her puppets and puppet theater in a Morristown designer showhouse. Designer Nancy Lee of Pittsford, New York, decorated the stateroom of the yacht *Timoneer* with Brunschwig's *Queen Anne Resist*. A fifty-two-foot Toledo, Ohio, boat was decorated by Nancy Cole with a wealth of well-loved Brunschwig chintzes,

Above: This glamorous hotel bedroom with a West Coast flavor was designed by Texeira, Inc. for the Beverly Wilshire Hotel — now the Regent Beverly Wilshire — using a special contract edition of *New Palissy* for curtains and large pillows on the bed.

Above, right: For the Four Seasons Resort Hotel in Nevis, in the West Indies, Frank Nicholson designed suites and this guest bedroom using *Les Roseaux Tropicaux* — meaning tropical rushes — a cotton printed in the United States with a Teflon finish. He chose three special contract colorways — green, pink, and blue. Eight colorways are available, and the print can be custom colored as well.

including *Mrs. Delany's Flowers* and *Mon Jardin*. And in Fort Lauderdale, Florida, Labbett North Design completely refurbished the yacht *Summertime* with Brunschwig fabrics. The list goes on and on, but the space for pictures has long run out!

Interior decoration affects everyone, and in turn it reflects the way we are — in our politics, technology, and spirit. America, more than almost anywhere else, is a country of continual change, and how we arrange our interior spaces echoes our ongoing development. Whether we live in a big city, in suburbia, or in the heart of the country, we are all affected daily by worldwide events; our décor alters with the times. We may feel the urge for complex, luxurious settings in one decade and for pared-down simplicity the next — but rest assured that there will always be a place for the great patterns like *Verrières*, *Le Lac*, and *Grand Génois*.

Linda Floyd designed this sophisticated bedroom suite for the Inn at Depot Hill, Capitola-by-the-Sea, California, using a black-and-white *Poligny* toile adapted from a French copperplate design. The crisp black border fences in the design and keeps it bandbox-neat.

The New York design firm of Irvine & Fleming customized this textured cotton damask for upholstery, embellishing it with an outline of deep red chain stitch, to blend into the English-inspired lounge of the New Albany Country Club in New Albany, Ohio.

Some Thoughts, Suggestions & Advice for Aspiring Interior Designers & Students ❧

An experienced interior decorator is Brunschwig's best ally. "Our collections are created with the designers and their clients in mind," affirms Murray Douglas. "We listen to their input and we want their reactions."

Residential *haut décor* means that curtaining, upholstery, papering, and paint work are all specially ordered for the customer. A designer can save an inexperienced client from making a lot of expensive mistakes.

Mrs. B. used to say that decorating is not just using luxurious sofa pillows and pleasing colors, but the building of a room. In the 1950s she advised, "You can create a sense of good architecture even in a house that has none, by your furniture arrangement. Don't put too many fabrics in a room. Decide on a main color and have at least three main pieces of furniture done alike. It makes the room quieter and holds it together. Chintzes and attractive prints are good anywhere, but they are especially important in houses without many fine things. Don't just create a pretty room. It's tragic not to put a personal imprint on your home." Mrs. B. had strong opinions about furniture as well: "Good antique pieces of furniture should not be upholstered any more often than is absolutely necessary," she'd say, "because the nail holes simply won't take the strain. But always use the best materials on antiques." She liked to mix various periods of furniture together, "though it takes a knowing hand." Her theory was "When you decorate, think in terms of architecture. Above all, observe, read, learn and inwardly digest."

Four decades later, many of these rules still apply, although the more you know, the more you can break away from convention and use your own creativity. Taste and style are always changing and evolving. Every ambitious designer wants to be part of that change.

Quality materials will last longer. The French may redecorate grand rooms only every twenty-five years or so because they are only used occasionally and they are traditionally done in the same style of textiles over and over again. Americans decorate more often, because they move from place to place, are more open to change, rarely live in serious historic houses, and can afford to (and want to show it). Also, American light is stronger and more damaging to textiles.

Brunschwig likes to encourage students, the designers of tomorrow. If they have a card from a school or college they can go to the showrooms, but it is best to go before ten o'clock in the morning or after four in the afternoon, when the salespeople are less busy. Avoid Wednesdays, when a lot of designers flock into the New York showroom. As a student you cannot take samples (large pieces) but you can take small cuttings.

Do ask intelligent questions. Brunschwig salespeople can and want to be helpful. "Our fabrics, wallpapers, trimmings, and furniture are known for being expensive, and the company is not responsible for the design job. If you are going to be a designer, *you* have to do that," insists Murray Douglas. "You know what you want for the end result, and you have to know the tools of the trade. Find good upholsterers, painters, contractors, and wallpaper hangers. They will be the most important allies you have. You will be the conduit for all the sources you use to complete the final product."

Get to know your salesperson in the showroom. The best salespeople follow up on everything. As the outspoken late decorator Jane Perin put it, "Design showroom salespeople are not decorators but expediters." Of her favorite Brunschwig salesman, Mr. Luciano Bini, she would say, "He doesn't have any taste at all . . . can't even match colors . . . and yet everybody wants him. He never lets anything go, you see. Good follower-upper. Goes right after it." To Mr. Bini, it's a lovely compliment!

On your first visit to a showroom, ask for someone to explain how the showroom is laid out, where the newest collection is displayed, and how samples and cuttings are requested. All Brunschwig showrooms are arranged according to type of design. For example, prints on linen are displayed in one group; glazed chintzes in another; and figured textures, damask, cut velvet, brocade, tapestry, and matelassé are hung together. Wallpapers are grouped by category — plains, panels, borders, stripes — subdivided into large scale, medium scale, and small scale.

Carry a notebook, pencil, and tape measure. Use the special services Brunschwig offers such as quilting, gaufrage, custom coloring, and embroidery. Be aware that some fabrics can be embroidered with soutache or fine cording or chain stitching to bring in needed color. Pay attention to the swatches attached to each fabric. Much thought has gone into Brunschwig's "scheming" ideas to show you the available coordinating, complementary fabrics and trimmings. This way you can save an amazing amount of time.

When a decorator sets up a business, he or she has to fill out an account application and a tax resale certificate in the showroom. The manager of each showroom is responsible for checking account applications. Brunschwig sells only to the trade, that is, designers and architects. Those who try to buy without having a genuine account are turned away. Years ago one couple came in and said they knew "Mr. and Mrs. Brunschwig" very well. It was clear they were interlopers, because no one who knew him *ever* said "Mr. Brunschwig." It was always "Colonel Brunschwig." Another would-be customer asked for "Mr. Fils," even pronouncing it

"Fills!" (By the by, Brunschwig & Fils is pronounced "brune shwig eh feese," to rhyme with "geese.")

European textile and decorating houses work differently from those in America. Anyone can walk in off the street and buy fabric, and decorators charge a flat, hourly fee. In America designers' fees are often included in the markup from wholesale to retail, and only the "trade" has access to the better fabric houses.

A word about caring for fabrics. No matter what you do, whether you put in special coated glass windows to stop ultraviolet rays or use lining and interlining (flannel or light-blocking or insulating material), all fabrics and wallpapers will eventually fade because of light. Solariums are particularly harsh on colorful fabrics. One solution is to use white textiles only, but all-white rooms are not easy to design — they look great in magazines, but you need beautiful textures and objects and wonderful space and proportions to offset the boredom of one color.

To protect upholstery, many people use slipcovers in summer when the sun is at its strongest. Slipcovers are a great idea to bring seasonal change, but they are nearly as expensive to make as more permanent-appearing upholstery. A good dressmaker who can sew slipcovers is invaluable. Don't fit them too tight — the relaxed look of a slipcover (called loose covers in England, where they were originally just sheets tucked over furniture) is considered far more stylish. Make sure that you have arm covers and antimacassars — the old-fashioned term for a cover on a high-backed armchair — made to match. A nice detail is to make an elastic-topped pocket in the side of a slipcover to hold a book, a magazine, or knitting or needlepoint. You can also have a slipcover made for a bed headboard, which can be easily whipped off when necessary. All these extra touches are great savings in the long run.

It's important to know something about the construction of textiles such as plain and compound weaves. Some basic information can be found in the Glossary, but scrutinize textiles for yourself whenever you get the opportunity. Designers of today are inspired by textured fabrics, chenilles, and damasks, and often use linen damask, which is less formal than the fancier silk ones. Damasks don't have to be traditional in design. There are all kinds of wonderful nontraditional patterns for modern designers looking for textures, and simple weaves like twills, chevrons, and dobbies can give maximum effect with an unpretentious look.

You may find yourself working in the "contract" area rather than in residential design. Contract work now usually refers to offices and banks, while its offshoots, "hospitality" and "health care" design, refer to hotel/restaurant and hospital/doctor office design. Commercial design usually requires large amounts of textiles in simplified patterns, with fewer colors to keep the costs down. The fabrics have to be hard-wearing and often have a synthetic content for strength. Fabric often has to be custom-made for the job. Contract work requires certain specifications, such as water-retarding treatments and fireproofing. Designers can save themselves many headaches if they find out at the beginning what the local and state requirements are before they confer with their Brunschwig contract salesperson.

There are some things the would-be decorator should know about wallpaper. On the side edges of all good wallpapers are plain white bands, like the selvedges on fabric. You will see an arrow and the word *TOP*, which indicates "This way up." You would be surprised how many times wallpaper is hung upside down, even by professionals! By the time it's up, it's too late. For tiny textured prints — such as *Peaweed*, a miniature version of the coral-inspired *Coraux* — paper hangers are advised to hang one panel up and the next down, to avoid a repetitious pattern forming and to guarantee a pleasing all-over effect.

You will also see the word *TRIM*. Good wallpapers are not trimmed before being shipped because the edges of the paper might get bruised — for safety there is a little selvedge band in case of damage. Good professional wallpaper hangers are used to trimming papers. If they refuse to trim the edges off — using a sharp blade and metal ruler — you've got somebody who's not a real pro.

Wallpaper is cut into single, double, and triple rolls by machine. It is most economical to buy triple rolls. In the price list of all good wallpaper suppliers you will find a chart to help you estimate the number of rolls needed. However, you are much better off letting your wallpaper hanger have a sample and look at the room to see where the openings are, so he or she can work out a more accurate estimate. Don't hold him to the last inch — always get extra, because there can be mistakes, and you may need more later for patching or covering switch plates (always a nice touch), and you can always use the excess for wrapping presents! Each roll is marked with the pattern number and the run number, which is very important if you have to order more. Be sure to order your wallpaper ahead of time, and examine it as soon as it is received to make sure you have ordered the correct pattern and colorway, before the paper hangers arrive. If the house has an attic, store extra wallpaper up there, where it is dry.

When talking to students, Murray Douglas tries to stress the importance of the museum habit, of visiting old and new exhibitions regularly. Sketching may be the best way to impress styles of rooms and furniture on one's memory. Mrs. Douglas is often surprised to discover that more students have been to Europe than have visited the Henry Francis du Pont Winterthur Museum in Delaware, "which seems unbelievable! I tell them to get on the train to Wilmington, spend two days with the best collection of decorative arts in this country." Seeing museums is important, as is going to showhouses. "Both are unreal in a way, but you learn what designers are currently thinking."

To get to know about furniture, go to antique shops, ask questions, and try to examine and handle antique furniture. This is the best way to learn whether a piece is genuinely old or a reproduction — something that cannot be taught in a classroom. One of the best books on the subject is *Authentic Decor* by Peter Thornton; it has an exciting collection of pictures, the illustrations are largely room portraits, and the text is well written and comprehensive. It is useful as a reference, as it combines interior design ideas and history — including political and technical developments, international trade, the brokering of important marriages, and the whole European scene — on a highly sophisticated level. "It wasn't until I got into the decorative arts that

Nancy Pierrepont designed this very English kind of morning room for a New York apartment using *Filigree* stripe with a moire pattern for walls and curtain.

history fell into place for me," admits Murray Douglas. "Then I began to understand what these tidal waves of political thought did to people — at least those who had the means to improve their surroundings aesthetically."

Begin your reference library now. Clip magazines and file them. Buy books and use them. Refine your filing system and make it a priority, not something for a rainy day!

Advice on Creating a First Home

Like her aunt, Mrs. B., Murray Douglas offers practical advice on decorating for young budgets:

- Your most important purchase will be a good sofa. It will last for twenty years or more. If you have room, buy a three-seater, which is great for naps and your growing family, and it really anchors a room.

- Work out your own floor plan with your existing furniture. Kits for planning are helpful tools, before you start shoving furniture around. Then don't be afraid to move furniture — it is often the first thing that a good decorator does. Use boxes to indicate placement of pieces you don't have. Eventually you'll find the best arrangement and traffic pattern for your way of life.

- When your floor plan is decided, then is the time to think about rugs. The carpet du jour — sisal — works with everything. If your floors are attractive, don't cover them completely. Rugs can delineate special areas. A rug can define a color scheme.

- If you don't have a dining room or don't want one, try to arrange a table conveniently close to the kitchen. This could be a table behind a sofa.

- If you don't have much upholstered furniture, create a draped table. This can be round, oblong, or square. It can become the room's focal point, with a lively fabric pattern on it — an old quilt, say, or a wild print, or an antique print. Top it with books, a lamp, and flowers.

- Bookcases give height to a room. Mirrors can too. Hang one over a chest for emphasis.

- Plan spaces for collections. Make tablescapes. Arrange objects so they have balance. "Balance leads to calm," says Stanley Barrows, who taught me at Parsons. He's right. Each group should be a composition.

- Buy simple vases and keep greenery in them if you can't afford flowers every week.

- For more daylight, leave curtains or draperies unlined and extend the rods beyond the window edge. But pull down the shades when direct sunlight comes in.

- If you can't afford curtains, use shades for privacy and light control. Unlined curtains hung on wooden rods and rings are easy to make.

- Identify the focal point of a room — a view, a fireplace, a painting, a piece of sculpture, a poster, or a found object. Group furniture around this point.

- For a bedroom without a great bedstead, or head-board, hang fabric matching the bedspread from the molding of the wall at the back of the bed.

I myself am not a practicing decorator. I find that using a decorator — Nan Heminway — saves me not only money but much wear and tear on the nerves. My advice — a layperson's advice — comes from observation. Rules can be broken in the right hands, forming fresh design ideas. This is how one era differs from another, and how style is born. More power to you all!

Murray Douglas's All-Time Favorite Fabrics 🐦

SMALL PRINTS

Coraux. The pattern carries color and goes with other prints. (See Chapter 1, p. 5.)

Peaweed. The best liner for beds, curtains, and walls. (See Marie Johnston's twins' nursery, Chapter 13, p. 150.)

PAISLEYS

Chatham. It is not too exotic, and always looks nice and easy. (See Chapter 10, p. 132.)

Cashemire. Though it comes in eight colorways, the red colorway is a classic.

TOILES

Trilport. It is very eighteenth-century French country house.

Thérèse, another classic, can be both simple and sophisticated.

West Indies. A documentary toile with a fresh feeling using botanical subject matter. (See Murray Douglas's own bedroom, Chapter 13, p. 148.)

Bromley Hall. An excellent reproduction of a copperplate classic. (See Chapter 1, p. 16.)

CHINTZES

Verrières. This pattern has inspired so many designers, for every room in the house. I want it for my city bedroom, in blue, of course. (See Chapter 1, pp. 25–27 and 88–89.)

Oriole. An early nineteenth-century botanical print that makes a wonderful companion to mahogany furniture.

Rivoli. One of our most successful brocade adaptations. It is very French in style, with ribbons and roses, but not cloying.

Tulip. Glazed chintz. A loosely drawn, large-scale pattern with lots of open ground.

LINEN PRINTS

Myrtille. This undemanding pattern, adapted from an embroidery, works well for curtains and upholstery.

Velay plaid. This design, developed from a Majorcan ikat, has good scale and a strong presence.

INDIENNES

Ménars bordered print. The contrast of the appliqué border and the sprigged field makes this an exciting design to work with. (See Chapter 1, p. 13.)

Grand Génois and its companion borders and filler. The grandfather of all chintzes is a dream to decorate with. My favorite is in a château bedroom belonging to Hubert de Givenchy. (See Chapter 1, p. 11.)

MY DREAM FABRIC

Duras. A hand-painted taffeta. Someday this will be in my boudoir! (I also love off-white *Richmond Dimity,* creamy matelassés, chenilles, and pale green damasks.)

Glossary 🔗

In the rarified and sometimes pretentious world of *haut décor*, French, English (as well as American), and Italian words are often used. Here is a list of useful decorating and technical terms that might help the reader.

all-over: Refers to a printed fabric or wallpaper that is fairly densely covered with a small, repeating pattern.

antimacassar: An old-fashioned term for a piece of crochet or cloth placed over the back of a high-backed chair to protect the upholstery (originally to protect it from Macassar oil, a hairdressing from Indonesia).

antique velvet: Unless it is *really* old, this is velvet that has been made to look distressed and older than it is.

arabesque: An Arab-inspired sinuous design. Arabesques developed into delicate, interlaced patterns of curlicues and traceries incorporating acanthus leaves, classical figures, urns, medallions, and/or grotesques based on Roman murals, paintings, and stucco reliefs. (Roman art was popularized in the eighteenth century by the "grand tours" of young British gentlemen of the time, by the discovery of Pompeii, and by the Adam brothers.) Arabesques were typical of many eighteenth- and early nineteenth-century designs.

Aristoloches: Seventeenth-century scroll patterns.

Aubusson: Handwoven carpet or tapestry with a distinctive style, named after the town in France where the style originated. Since the carpets are made with a tapestry weave, they are typically flat.

azulejos: Distinctive Portuguese tiles, often blue and white with complex designs.

baldachin: A high, draped crown-shaped structure over a bed, dais, or throne. From the Italian, *baldacchino*.

banyan: Indian name for a man's at-home robe or dressing gown, from the eighteenth century.

batik: A patterned fabric produced by coating areas not to be dyed with wax. Originally from Indonesia.

bengaline: A lustrous fabric with ribs made from heavy cords in the filling.

bergère: A large, deep armchair with closed arms and a seat cushion.

block fringe: Usually a straight-cut fringe in blocks of color. (It is sometimes seen with a more delicate, fan-shaped edge.)

block printing: Hand printing using wood blocks onto which a design has been carved. The blocks are coated from a dye pad and applied to cloth. (Somewhat similar to potato or linoleum printing done in school.)

blotch print: A printing effect whereby the ground area (which can be quite large) is colored as well as the patterned area.

boiserie: Decorative wood carving, especially paneling.

box pleats: Pleats that turn in alternate directions, forming a series of "boxes" between inverted pleats.

brocading: An elaborate form of weaving to create an embroidered effect. Usually silk or metal threads are wrapped around the warp threads to form raised designs, but an example of wool-brocaded linen can be seen on the Francis chair in Chapter 1,

p. 18. (See *lampas* for comparison.)

brocatelle: A sculptured, low-relief Jacquard pattern in a satin weave. A brocatelle is always backed for strength by extra-filling yarns of cotton or linen, which do not appear on the surface of the fabric but give the raised effect.

café curtains: Simple unlined curtains covering the bottom part of a window.

canapé: A small sofa (not an hors d'oeuvre!) introduced under Louis XIV, usually en suite with armchairs — bergères or fauteuils.

carpet: (See *rugs*.) In America, carpeting is bought by the yard to be used wall to wall. "Area rugs" are individual carpets. In England, polite (old-fashioned) society talks about "Oriental carpets," not "Oriental rugs." Choose your own expression accordingly. Oriental carpets were often called "Turkey carpets" in the past.

chain stitch: An embroidery stitch formed from one continuous thread. The very first sewing machines made this stitch, which can be pulled out easily if you find the end of the thread.

chaîne: A French word meaning the warp on a loom.

chambray: A cotton shirting named after the French town, Cambrai, where the cloth was originally made.

chenille: A fabric made using chenille yarn, which is fuzzy like a caterpillar (from the French word for caterpillar).

chevron: A twill weave going in different directions to create a herringbone effect.

chiné: Literally, "made Chinese," but the term came to be used by the French for anything exotic, especially warp-dyed fabrics.

chintz: Printed cotton fabric used almost exclusively in interior decoration; it often has a glazed finish (from an Indian word).

chou: A crumpled puff of fabric used to accent curtain swags, or at the top and/or bottom of chandelier-chain covers, or on overhead bed drapery (from the French for "cabbage").

ciselé velvet: A combination of cut and uncut velvet (from the French for sculptured or chiseled). On figured voided ciselé velvet the pile is limited to part of the fabric face. The pile is not actually cut away from these areas but is woven into the fabric back. (See also *devoré velvet*.)

colorway: The number of colors, or color variations, in which a fabric can be purchased.

commercial match: Colors that match to a degree acceptable in a decorating scheme.

compound weaves: Fabrics with more than one warp and more than one filling. Some, such as brocaded ottoman or a combination of damask and brocading, can be very complex, requiring a month just to set up the loom. (And skilled French craftspeople cannot be rushed! If they fall ill, you have to wait until they get better!)

contract work: A trade term for nonresidential interior design. The term now applies mainly to offices and banks. (See also *hospitality* and *health care*, which are specific types of contract work.)

converter: The person or business responsible for converting greige goods into finished, printed fabric.

cording: Twisted or braided cord in a number of sizes and variations, either applied to or inserted into upholstery and cushion or pillow edges to add color and definition. When cording becomes over an inch in diameter, it is often referred to as rope — such as the rope held up by brass stands to bar the way in decorators' showhouses, cinemas, and so on.

corduroy: Any one of many variations of velvety-pile fabrics woven into vertical ribs, or wales, and then cut. Uncut corduroy has a ribless pile (from the French *corde du roi* — originally it was a very regal fabric).

crewel: Designs based on a certain type of late-seventeenth-century English embroidery using wool on unbleached linen or cotton. The patterns usually combine leaves, vines, flowers, and animals.

croquis: A sketched or painted idea for a print.

curtains: The more haut décor term for window coverings — though one can also talk about "draperies" or even use the old-fashioned term *a draper* for one who purveys such fabrics. (See also *drapes*.)

cushions: British and American haut décor term for a "throw pillow" tossed on furniture; many Americans use the term *cushion* for a thick seat pad on upholstered sofas and armchairs.

cut velvet: Technically, velvet with a soft pile is "cut." Pile-on-pile velvet has a sculptured appearance produced by weaving the velvet with two different piles. *Cut velvet* is often used to describe voided velvet, which is woven to have some areas with pile and some with no pile. (See also *ciselé velvet*, *devoré velvet*, *figured velvet*, *gaufrage*, *pile-on-pile velvet*, and *voided velvet*.)

dado: The lower part of an interior wall, below the chair rail; especially when it is decorated in contrast to the upper wall.

damask: A fabric named after the Syrian city of Damascus, created by combining two weaves, twill and satin. Check it by seeing if the reverse has satin in the place of twill, and twill in the place of satin. Damask is reversible and limited to two colors — warp and weft threads.

decorator (interior): The old-fashioned, more traditional term for an interior designer. Though the term is sometimes used in a derogatory way, many haut décor firms prefer to be called interior decorators (though they do use the term designer from time to time), because they are usually secure in their own knowledge and position and are generally best known for their residential work. In England, among those who do not use a professional decorator, the term *decorator* can also apply to a house painter. (See also *designer*.)

découpage: A design formed from cutout and rearranged pieces of a material (usually paper).

designer (interior): The more general term for a professional decorator; what interior design schools turn out. It refers to both residential and commercial designers. Pick the label most suited to you. (See also *decorator*.)

devoré velvet: Velvet pile on fine mesh with the pile

Eveline Peardon frames a window in the "borning room" of the Peardon's Connecticut house with an *indienne* print.

burned away in areas to form three-dimensional patterns; used mainly for clothing, as it is rather fragile for most decorative uses.

dimity: A heavy everyday cloth in the eighteenth century; a medium-weight fabric in the nineteenth century; a lightweight, unpretentious fabric today. Dimity usually has a patterned weave, most often vertical ribs.

Directoire: A style in France during the early years of Bonaparte's power (1795–99), before Napoléon became Emperor.

district check: A houndstooth check with a larger, contrasting check dividing it (named by Scottish tweed makers).

dobby: A weave requiring special loom adjustments to produce small, symmetrical, repeating motifs. Named for the English "dobby boy," who sat atop the loom and lifted the warp threads (from *dobbin*, a term for a workhorse).

documentary: In fabric or wallpaper terms, this is a print based on a proven historical design.

drapes: A shortened term for draperies. Though many Americans use the term *drapes* when they refer to window curtains, grand decorators might think it somewhat common. You decide. Murray Douglas says the term *drapes* always makes her think of church entrances draped in crepe for funerals!

draw loom: A loom invented in the first centuries A.D. It utilized a treadle mechanism to raise each warp thread independently by a string attached above the loom, leaving both hands free to pass the shuttle.

drugget: In England, common cloth, once known as linsey-woolsey. In the eighteenth century it was a wool or mixed fabric used for clothes. The nineteenth-century version was very wide — two to four yards — and was laid on top of carpets to protect them or as padding under them or as a cheap, substitute floor covering.

dupion: Strong slubbed silk formed from double cocoons called dupions.

dust ruffles: Gathered or straight lengths of fabric that hang from below the mattress to the floor on a well-dressed bed.

dye lots: Batches of printed or dyed fabric. Sometimes colors vary slightly from one dye lot to another. (See *run number*.)

embossing: A design pressed into fabric with heat, rather like making a waffle. (See *gaufrage*.)

embroidery: Many ways of embellishing fabric with applied colored or white thread. Embroidery is done by hand or by machine. The many types include appliqué, bead-work, crewel, cut-work, drawnwork (also called hemstitching or faggoting), eyelet embroidery (called broderie anglaise in England and France), needlepoint (see also *gros point* and *petit point*), quilting, smocking, stump-work (called Berlin-work in the nineteenth century), and more. Surface stitches include back stitch, chain stitch, French knots, herringbone stitch, lazy daisy, satin stitch, and more.

Empire: Often pronounced "Om-peer." A style in France when Napoléon was Emperor (1804–1815), roughly around the time of the Regency in England and the Federal period in the United States. Design motifs include bees, Roman details, stripes, tents, and the neoclassic look. There is also the Second Empire style, which is florid in comparison, from when, as far as style was concerned, Empress Eugénie and her couturier, Worth, ruled Paris (1852–70).

enfilade: A series of rooms — or other things — leading from one to the next in a straight line. Decorators love this word, although American decorators often use the term *shotgun* for the same effect on a less pretentious scale.

en suite: A decorating scheme that uses the same fabric on walls and curtains, and sometimes also on upholstery, bed hangings, and bed covers.

faille: A fine, horizontally ribbed fabric with a sheen and a heavier rib in the filling; has a formal, evening-gown look.

fall-on: A term used to describe one color overprinting another, as in yellow printed on blue to create green.

fan edging: Loop-fringed braids inserted or applied to a fabric, giving it a distinctive wavy effect; it can be colored in blocks.

fauteuil: An armchair (a French word).

faux: Painted effects that simulate real materials (from the French for "false"). Faux bois is "false wood," faux marbre is "false marble," or a marbleized surface.

felt: A fabric formed by matting fibers — usually wool — under heat and pressure.

figured velvet: A patterned velvet with a design formed by cut and uncut loops.

finial: A knob used on the top of lamps to hold the shade in place, or on the top of bedposts, or on the ends of curtain rods (where they may look like decorators' hand grenades).

flatbed printing: A mechanized method of printing wherein the fabric moves on a belt, while the printing screens remain stationary.

French corners: Gathering or pleating at the corners of cushions and pillows to give a soft, rounded effect.

Furniture makers use the terms *butterfly corners* and *gathered corners*, and they are sometimes called Turkish corners.

frisé: A firm fabric with a pile of uncut loops (from the French word meaning "curled"); also called *frieze*.

fugitive: A dye or print that runs when washed or fades in sunlight.

gamme: Colored squares outside the trim line of wallpaper and on the selvedge of printed fabric that show the number of colors used (from the French for "scale" or "gamut").

gathering: A term for fabric that is stitched so that it puckers to give fullness; also called shirring.

gaufrage: A process whereby fabric is embossed with a heated weight to create a pattern (from the Flemish for "waffle").

gimp: A flat, narrow (usually between three eighths to one half inch wide) woven trimming that comes in a variety of raised patterns; often used on wood-frame furniture to cover upholstery tacks, but also used in many decorative ways on walls, edges of lamp shades, and pillows.

giselles: A French term for supple silk fringes that create a soft zigzag effect; often called fan-edge fringes in America.

glazed: A term used to describe a glossy fabric surface, produced by heat, heavy pressure, chemical action, or a glazing substance.

Gobelins: The name of a French state tapestry firm in Paris, founded under Henri IV and still going strong.

goods: Usually refers to material, cloth, stuff, or fabric.

Gothic; Gothick: The former refers to architectural forms of the Middle Ages, such as pointed arches, trefoils, crockets, and flying buttresses, implying the barbaric quality of the Goths as opposed to the classic Greek and Roman pillared temple forms. Eighteenth-century architectural dilettantes fantasized Gothic Revival forms into Gothick, frequently using lighthearted plaster and wood instead of brute stone.

grain: The true warp, or direction of vertical threads, of a fabric. This can be established by pressing a pin and running it down on the fabric, or by measuring in from the selvedge.

greige goods: Pronounced "gray." Plain, unfinished goods for printing.

grisaille: A pattern in tones of gray or sepia, sometimes used on wallpaper to give the illusion of sculpture.

grosgrain: A ribbed fabric; also a ribbed ribbon.

gros point: A needlework effect, larger than *petit point*. It can be imitated on fabrics.

grotesques: From the word "grotto," decorative patterns not unlike arabesque curlicues, using Italian Baroque–inspired details such as human figures, animal forms, and masks.

ground: The field or background of a pattern.

hand blocking: A fabric printing process wherein wooden blocks are carved with a pattern, charged from a dye pad, and pressed by hand onto cloth to produce the design. Hand blocking means something completely different when it refers to hatmaking, needlepoint, or knitting. (See *Chapter 1*.)

hand printing: Originally this meant a design manually printed by flat screens; but the term now includes simulated hand-screen printing, which allows for drying time between each color (printing "wet on dry").

handwoven: Woven by hand rather than by a power-driven machine loom.

head colors: The colors in a printed design that form the pattern. The background is called the blotch.

health care: A trade term for interior design of hospitals and health care offices.

heddles: A device on a loom, worked by a foot pedal, that lifts the warp yarns so the shuttle can be passed through.

herringbone: A weave in which twills, or diagonal weaves, alternate directions, forming a zigzag pattern.

horsehair: A cloth, used extensively in the eighteenth and nineteenth centuries, with a weft made of hair from horses' tails. Real horsehair fabric is therefore only about twenty-one inches wide. Now there are good synthetic horsehairs that come in standard widths.

hospitality: A trade term for interior design of restaurants, inns, hotels, and other spaces where the public is housed or entertained.

imberlines: A type of fabric with a woven, striped ground and a large damask pattern; used since the eighteenth century for upholstery and wall hangings.

ikat: Warp-dyed fabrics, originally from Indonesia, India, and Afghanistan. The warp is printed or tie-dyed before weaving. (See *chiné.*)

indiennes: Fabrics inspired by India. The first colorful, painted cottons were produced in India; when they were imported into France they were called *indiennes.*

interlining: A fabric inserted between the front and the lining of curtains (or coverlets or table skirts) to provide body or insulation and/or to prevent light from coming through.

jabot: Pronounced "jah-boh." In curtain making, vertical folds of fabric, often draped to reveal contrasting undersides.

Jacquard weaving: Method of weaving large patterned designs using punched cards, named after the Frenchman Joseph-Marie Jacquard (1752–1834). Weavers, fearing for their jobs, burned his invention when it was first fitted to Lyon's looms in 1812. Eventually they accepted it as better, faster, and a good thing for all. Jacquard fabrics are those woven on a Jacquard loom.

jasmins: A French passementerie term for chains of tiny silk-covered loops and flowerlike motifs.

jaspé: A word used by some English textile makers to describe an effect similar to *strié,* a fine, uneven, textured vertical stripe pattern. *Strié* was originally made by dripping dye down fabric or paper.

knife edge: A term used to describe seat pads and pillows with no inserts of fabric to add thickness to the shape.

knife edge pleats: Pleats of any size that all turn in one direction.

knockoff: A slang term for an unauthorized copy of a pattern or style (usually a cheaper version).

lace: Fine open-work fabric or edging often made from thread, or cut and embroidered. The many varieties of lace include Alençon lace, Chantilly lace, Cluny lace, guipure lace, Irish lace, Nottingham lace, Scottish lace, Val lace, Venise lace, tatting, and more.

lamé: A fabric made with metallic thread or synthetic metallic thread.

lampas: A compound woven cloth with figured patterns, bulkier than a true brocaded cloth because all the additional wefts are bound into the fabric and carried from selvedge to selvedge.

leading edges: The edges of curtains that come together when the curtains are closed.

lock stitch: A stitch that is often used to outline fabric designs on quilts. Unlike a chain stitch, a lock stitch will not pull out in one thread if it catches on jewelry or a cat's claw.

looseback: Refers to soft, upholstered furniture with separately made seat back cushions. Tightback furniture has cushioning built into the back.

machine print: Patterns printed by machine rather than by hand.

madder: A natural dye made from a plant, formerly used to create colors ranging from aubergine to pink.

matelassé: A double-woven textile with a quilted appearance.

mezzaro: Italian term for a large printed square or rectangular shawl worn by women in Genoa, a center of fabric printing since the late eighteenth century. *Mezzari* were often based on Indian tree of life designs. Brunschwig's *Grand Génois* probably gets its name from the European familiarity with *mezzari.* Brunschwig's *Beauport Promenade,* a design used on both fabric and wallpaper, was based on a *mezzaro.*

moiré: Fabric with a watered-silk appearance. Originally produced by applying huge pressure from heated cylinders; now available in woven or printed versions. The French term is *moirage.*

mordant: A chemical that fixes dyes, making printed cloth washable and the dye colorfast.

moreen: A plain worsted weave, usually wool, with a weft heavier than the warp, which gives it a ribbed effect. Can be moiréd or embossed to simulate damask. (See Chapter 1, p. 21.)

moss fringe: A silky, fringed braid, usually inserted, with a cut edge. It often looks most effective when the fringe is doubled and therefore fuller.

mull: A fine, sheer fabric, usually cotton but sometimes silk.

nail heads: Large-headed metal nails, sometimes brass, sometimes with fancy designs, used to hold fabric to a wooden chair frame.

nap: The direction in which the pile of a fabric is brushed, especially on velvets. (See *pile*, p. 187.)

noisettes: A passementerie term for small, decorative nutshapes covered in silk threads.

Norwich stripe: Colorful English wool stripe, often figured, with an ombré effect in the warp. An example is Brunschwig's *Pennypacker* stripe, which was based on a document at the Winterthur Museum.

ombré: A shaded effect (French for "shadowed").

one way: A printed pattern that has one direction that is definitely "up."

ottoman: A fabric with a silky ribbed effect that runs from selvedge to selvedge. Technically the fabric requires two warps to produce ribs of unequal widths. An ottoman is also a large padded footstool, often used with an upholstered armchair.

paisley: A design based on the Indian cone motif, named after Paisley, Scotland, where soft wool shawls using variations of these patterns were produced, to copy the more expensive originals made in Kashmir, India.

palampore: An Indian word for coverlet; also, a hanging typically patterned with a large tree of life motif, such as Brunschwig's *Grand Génois*. (See Chapter 1, pp. 10–11.)

passementerie: Any type of cord, braid, fringe, or tassel, used for embellishment. Can range from a simple edging to an elaborate handmade two-thousand-dollar-a-yard confection.

patina: In fabrics, an antiqued look, sometimes achieved through age and sometimes contrived. (See also *antique velvet*.)

pelmet: A decorative band, drape, or ruffle used to hide the pulley system on curtains. (See also *valance*.)

penciled blue: A process used for early *indienne* designs in which indigo dye was "penciled" (painted) on top of yellow to produce green.

piece-dyed: Fabric that is dyed after it is woven. A "piece" is a fifty-yard length of fabric.

pile: A velvety surface formed by raised loops that are cut and sheared. (See also *nap*.)

pile-on-pile velvet: Velvet with two pile heights woven to create a pattern. (See also *voided velvet* and *ciselé velvet*.)

pillows: See *cushions*.

pinch pleats: Groups of pleats at the top of a curtain. There are many variations, some formed using commercial pleating tape and others stitched individually.

piping: See *welt*.

platform: The horizontal area of a chair or sofa that seat pads or cushions sit on.

plate printing: A process wherein engraved plates are used to print single-colored toiles. Originally the plates were flat; today metal cylinders are used to speed printing. Also called copper plate printing.

plissé: A seersucker effect obtained by loom tension or by heat pressing.

plush: Velvet with a very high pile.

point rentré: A weaving technique, invented early in the eighteenth century by Jean Revel, which allows colors to shade into one another for greater naturalism.

pongee: Usually refers to a type of unbleached, plain-weave silk.

portière: A curtain hanging on a door or across a doorway to cut drafts.

power loom: A loom operated by mechanical means, not by hand.

puddle: The amount by which a curtain or table cover flows onto the floor. Can vary from one to eight inches — more than that is excessive.

railroading: A method by which goods are cut down the grain, as opposed to the orthodox method of cutting across the grain and then matching the print on each seam. Railroading is useful for nondirectional fabrics to save needless seams.

récamier: a neoclassic sofa for reclining, made fashionable by Mme. Récamier, a great beauty at the time of Napoléon's empire. Mme. Récamier was portrayed on such a sofa by the equally fashionable French painter Jacques-Louis David (pronounced "Da-veed").

Régence: A French style, from the period when Philippe duc d'Orléans was regent after Louis XIV's death and before Louis XV reached his maturity (1715–23), a period of suppleness and grace in the decorative arts.

rep or repp: A fine-ribbed fabric, often used for striped ties.

repeat: The length of a printed or woven pattern, before it repeats itself. A large repeat is always more expensive to use because more cloth is required to match the print on a curtain or on furniture.

resist print (or dye): A method of creating a pattern by covering certain areas before dyeing, often with wax, which is then removed after dyeing. A series of dye baths can be used to create multicolored designs.

rosette: A decorative circular confection made of fabric or ribbon, used to punctuate draperies.

rotary screen printing: A mechanized form of screen printing, wherein dye is forced through a cylindrical drum onto moving fabric.

rouge d'Andrinople: The French phrase for Turkey red — named after the Middle Eastern city.

rug: In America, almost any carpet of a fixed size is referred to as a rug. If large, it would be called a carpet in England. A rug in England is usually something that might be put in front of the fireplace, placed by a bedside, or used as a traveling blanket. (See also *carpet.*)

run number: The number of a specific printing of a wallpaper — similar to a dye lot for fabrics.

sateen: A cotton fabric in a satin weave.

satin weave: A weave in which the warp is of the most precious threads, such as silk, and covers the weft in order to produce a reflective, lustrous effect.

screen engraver: The artist-craftsman who translates a design onto a screen (an important person in the art of fabric printing).

screen printing: In today's printing terms, a process in which rotary screens are used for each color. The fabric moves quickly under the screens, not allowing for drying time. Also called wet-on-wet printing.

seat pads: Pads of varying thickness used to soften a chair seat or to protect a cane seat. (See also *squab.*)

self fabric: Matching fabric, such as for the welt on a chair or cushion, cut from the same cloth as the object.

selvedge: The woven edges of a piece of cloth. On a printed decorative fabric, this is where you often find the name of the company that created it, a color *gamme* indicating the number of screens used to print it, and arrows pointing out the up and down directions of its design.

shantung: A form of slubbed silk, usually unbleached.

slub: Fibers are slubbed when they vary from thin to thick and this creates a texture in the weave.

sociable: A circular sofa popular in the nineteenth century.

soutache: A narrow braid, originally used on military uniforms, usually top-stitched on in a central groove (from the Hungarian *sujtás*).

squab: An English term for a removable seat pad on a chair.

strié: A fine, uneven vertical stripe. (See also *jaspé.*)

strike-offs: Test tries of print colors in print mills.

sunburst pleats: Concertina pleats radiating in size so that they widen toward the outer edge.

swag: Generally refers to a looping fold of fabric used in draping curtains.

tabby: The simplest over-and-under weave, such as children use to make pot holders in kindergarten; also called a plain weave.

taffeta: A plain weave made by using warp and filling yarns of equal weight, producing a firm, close weave. We tend to think of it as a crisp, silklike fabric, but it is really a weave. Cotton taffeta is a very useful decorative fabric.

tête-à-tête: An S-shaped divan (from the French, meaning "head-to-head" or "intimate").

tiebacks: Devices used to hold curtains back in a graceful loop. There are many different types; they can be made of self fabric, metal, or passementerie (called an *embrasse* in French).

tightback: Refers to soft, upholstered furniture in which the back cushioning is part of the piece. Looseback means the cushions are separate and can be removed from the back.

toile: A monotone print with an intricate, engraved quality, often of a historical, pictorial subject. The name is short for *toile de Jouy;* Jouy is a town in France where many famous toiles were printed.

ton-sur-ton: French for "tone-on-tone," such as dark beige on light beige.

trapunto: A decorative, linear, quilted design made by stitching through two layers and trapping soft cotton cords underneath to form a pattern.

tree of life: A classic Indian pattern of a flowering tree. The design has been adapted in many ways and for many things — including fabrics and china — over the centuries.

treillage: A trellis pattern, usually formed of diagonal crisscrosses. Can refer to a trellis effect on fabric or wallpaper.

trim: A border allowance on either edge of printed wallpaper, like selvedges on fabrics, that protects the edges from damage in shipping and has to be trimmed off before the paper is hung. Also refers to passementerie.

tufting: A method of upholstering using buttons or decorative knots to hold the fabric covering the deep padding in place.

Turkish corners: See *French corners.*

Turk's head: A globe-shaped, decorative, handmade knot formed from cord or fabric tubing.

tussah: A rough type of silk with slubs from uncultivated silkworms.

twill: A diagonal, stepped weave.

undercurtains: Unlined curtains of a sheer fabric, used in conjunction with heavier, more decorative curtains to preserve privacy but let in light.

valance: Another term for a pelmet; a very short curtain or heading that hides the curtain rings or pulling system.

vermicelli: Small, continuous curly lines in a design (from the Italian for "worms").

voided velvet: Jacquard-patterned fabric with areas having a velvet pile contrasting with areas without pile, giving a sculptured effect.

warp: The threads that run down a fabric. These threads are first set up on a loom, and the weft threads are then woven in. (See also *weft.*)

warp-printing: A method of printing in which a pattern is first printed, painted, or tie-dyed on the warp, and then a plain filler is woven in, producing a softened effect with a slightly fuzzy edge. (See also *ikat.*)

wax print: A fabric produced by applying wax in a pattern onto cloth, dipping the cloth into dye, and then removing the wax, leaving the original uncolored cloth beneath. (See also *batik, resist.*)

weft: The threads that weave across the warp from selvedge to selvedge; sometimes called the filling or the woof.

welt: Fabric cut in bias strips, filled with cording, and then stitched between seams to give contrast or emphasis to slipcovers or upholstery. Also known as piping. *Self welt* is used to indicate when the fabric and the welt match. Double-welting is a less expensive way to trim upholstered furniture because the nail heads can be hidden between the welts; single welts must be hand-sewn.

window treatments: A term that refers to everything to do with windows, including the drapery of the curtains and their fabrics, linings, interlinings, pelmets (or valances), undercurtains, rods, rings, finials, tiebacks, and so on.

yarn-dyed fabric: Fabric made from yarns dyed before they are made into cloth. Yarn-dyed fabric is superior to piece-dyed fabric because the threads are completely and individually covered in dye.

Selected Bibliography 🌿

BOOKS

Adams, Michael Henry. *American Regional Rooms: A New Perspective on Traditional Design*. New York: Mallard Press, 1992.

Andréani, Carole. *La Passementerie*. Paris: À l'initiative de l'Association "Métiers d'art de Paris" et de la Mairie de Paris en collaboration avec la Chambre Syndicale des Textiles d'Ameublement, 1993.

Baldwin, Billy. *Billy Baldwin Decorates*. New York: Holt, Rinehart and Winston, 1972.

———. *Billy Baldwin Remembers*. New York: Harcourt Brace Jovanovich, 1974.

Boudet, Pierre; and Bernard Gomond. *La Passementerie*. Paris: Dessain et Tolra, 1981.

Boudet, Pierre; Paul Dô; and Bernard Gomond. *Des Dorelotiers aux Passementeriers*. Paris: Union Centrale des Art Décoratifs, 1973.

Brédif, Josette. *Printed French Fabrics: Toiles de Jouy*. New York: Rizzoli, 1989.

Brown, Erica. *Sixty Years of Interior Design: The World of McMillen*. New York: Viking, 1982.

Burnham, Dorothy K. *Warp & Weft: A Textile Terminology*. Toronto: Royal Ontario Museum. The Hunter Rose Company, 1980.

Calloway, Stephen. *Twentieth-Century Decoration: The Domestic Interior from 1900 to the Present Day*. London: Weidenfeld & Nicolson, 1988.

Carr, William H. A. *The du Ponts of Delaware: A Fantastic Dynasty*. New York: Dodd, Mead & Company, 1964.

Cooper, Wendy H. *Classical Taste in America: 1800–1840*. Baltimore: Abbeville, 1993.

A Dictionary of Textile Terms. Danville, Virginia: Dan River, 1971.

Hamlin, Talbot. *Greek Revival Architecture in America*. New York: Dover, 1964.

Jones, Chester. *Colefax & Fowler: The Best in English Interior Decoration*. Boston: Bulfinch Press, 1989.

Lynn, Catherine. *Wallpaper in America: From the Seventeenth Century to World War I*. New York: W. W. Norton, 1980.

Mayhew, Edgar de N.; and Minor Myers, Jr. *A Documentary History of American Interiors: From the Colonial Era to 1915*. New York: Scribners, 1980.

The wallpaper in a guest room in the Peardon's house in Connecticut is *Summerhouse trellis*.

Montgomery, Florence M. *Textiles in America, 1650–1870*. New York: W. W. Norton, 1984.

Nicolson, Nigel. *Great Houses of Britain*. London: Weidenfeld and Nicolson, 1965.

Nylander, Jane C. *Fabrics for Historic Buildings*. Rev. ed. Washington, D.C.: The Preservation Press, National Trust for Historic Preservation, 1990.

Nylander, Richard C. *Wallpapers for Historic Buildings*. Rev. ed. Washington, D.C.: The Preservation Press, National Trust for Historic Preservation, 1992.

Oman, Charles C.; and Jean Hamilton. *Wallpapers: An International History and Illustrated Survey*. New York: Harry N. Abrams, 1982.

Peterson, Harold L. *Americans at Home*. New York: Charles Scribner's Sons, 1971.

Praz, Mario. *Interior Decoration: An Illustrated History from Pompeii to Art Nouveau*. New York: Thames and Hudson, 1982.

Sandwith, Hermione; and Sheila Stainton. *The National Trust Manual of Housekeeping*. London: Viking, 1964.

Slavin, Richard E., III. *Opulent Textiles: The Schumacher Collection*. New York: Crown, 1992.

Smith, C. Ray. *Interior Design in Twentieth-Century America: A History*. New York: Harper & Row, 1987.

Thornton, Peter. *Authentic Decor: The Domestic Interior, 1620–1920*. London: Weidenfeld & Nicolson, 1984.

Tracy, Berry B. *Federal Furniture and Decorative Arts at Boscobel*. New York: Harry N. Abrams, 1981.

Wall, Charles C.; Christine Meadows; John H. Rhodehamel; and Ellen McCalister Clark. *Mount Vernon: A Handbook*. Ed. Catherine Fallen. Mount Vernon, Virginia: The Mount Vernon Ladies Association, 1985.

Wingate, Dr. Isobel B. *Fairchild's Dictionary of Textiles*. 6th ed. New York: Fairchild Publications, 1979.

PAMPHLETS AND PERIODICALS

D'Arnoux, Alexandra. "Kingpin: An All-in-the-Family Affair," *Maison et Jardin/Vogue Décoration*, 37–8.

Bernier, Rosamond. "Palm Beach Fable," *House & Garden* (May 1984), 118–28.

Brunschwig, Zelina. "Fabrics with Companion Wallpapers! Today's Answer to a Decorator's Prayer," *The Interior Decorators' and Contract News* (January 1964), 10.

Hunter, Sarah Johnston. "A Designing Woman: Alumna Ross Johnson Francis," *Salem Academy Alumnae Magazine* (Spring 1989).

Interiors, January 1973. Colonel Brunschwig's obituary.

Iovine, Julie V. "Books in the Belfry," *The New York Times Magazine* (January 23, 1994), 44–6.

Louie, Elaine. "A Teacher Who Lives His Lesson of Design," *New York Times* (November 25, 1993).

Mackie, Joan. "Return to Forever," *Canadian House & Home* (May 1987), 46–51.

Meadows, Christine. "The Furniture," *Antiques* (February 1989), 480–89.

Mosca, Matthew John. "The House and Its Restoration," *Antiques* (February 1989), 472.

Passell, Susan. "Contract Work Brings New Dimension," *Home Furnishings Daily* (March 7, 1967).

Reagan, Michele. "Train Travels in Style," *Specifyer's Guide* (1990), 12–14.

Scott, Barbara. "Intricate Arcadias," *Country Life* (June 8, 1993), 64–5.

Scott, Ellen. "Institute Exhibits First Museum Fabric Show," Albany *Times Union* (March 9, 1962), 18.

———. "Personalize Your Home, Says Decorator," Albany *Times Union* (March 13, 1962), 18.

Slesin, Suzanne. " 'Trade Only!' Walls Weaken." *New York Times* (July 15, 1993), C 1, C 6.

Tassel, Janet. "Viva I Tatti." *Harvard Magazine* (March–April 1994), 34–41.

Vespa, Mary. "Patterned after History," *Colonial Homes* (April 1993).

The Interior Decorators' and Contract News (September 1965), "What's New for Decor; News in Fabric and Walls."

Acknowledgments

Of the Brunschwig personnel, first and foremost our thanks goes to Brunschwig's president, Thomas P. Peardon, for his advice and patience, and his wife, Eveline, who not only provided us with fabulous meals in the French tradition but also checked French spelling and usage. Also thanks to Jean Chognard, Colonel Brunschwig's nephew, who loaned letters and verified family data.

Special thanks to Shirley Kelly, Mrs. Douglas's assistant, whose eagle eye was essential; she corrected inaccuracies and had the unenviable task of overseeing the return of hundreds of photographs to their rightful owners. Thanks to Judy Straeten for valuable and professional archival information. For answering endless questions and tracking down queries, thanks to Ross Francis, Dorothy Magnani, Sara Labas, Stephen Dahlquist, John Barker, and especially Paul Dobrowolski, who was wonderfully hospitable to us on Nantucket. Thanks to the staff at North White Plains, including Patrick Mongiello, Nancy Weir, Lewis Paul, and Thomas Marshall for answering questions; and to Mr. Peardon's assistant, Joëlle Tessier; and to Regina King for checking names of Brunschwig products. Also thanks to the public relations people, Susan Becher and her writer, Akiko Busch.

It is unfair to single out any of the showroom representatives, especially those who sent photographs and recommended designers, but we would like to mention those with whom we had the most contact: Carmie Dennis, Marcia Doering, Valerie Aikin, David Cutler, Dolores Brucklmaier, and Michael Petrie.

A big and affectionate thank you to the third member of our troika, our traveling photographer, Alex McLean, a companion who kept cool under fire, drove like a dream, and was always fun to work with. As you will see, he took some pretty good photographs too.

An especial thanks to Albert Hadley for writing such a glowing introduction.

Thanks also to Chippy's agent, Angela Miller, who started the ball rolling, and to Robert Cousins, who encouraged Murray Douglas, and reassured the Brunschwig powers-that-be that this book was a worthy project to attempt.

At Little, Brown/Bulfinch Press, thanks to Lindley Boeghold, the editor first assigned to the job, and an even bigger thanks to Dorothy Williams, the editor who took it over, and to her editorial assistant, Janice O'Leary. Also thanks to Susan Marsh, who designed the book.

Thanks to Ethel (Mrs. Everett) Smith, the late Jane Perin, and Louis Bowen, who, as close friends of the late Mrs. Brunschwig, told wonderful tales of her career. Grateful thanks to Diana Calamari of Burke's Ltd. for lending antiques.

Thanks to all the people who gave us shelter when needed: Robin and Jacqueline Basker, Betsy Frankel, Robert L. Hunker, Sue Lankenau, Merlin Pennink, John Reed, Bill and Mary Scanlon, Imogen Taylor, Mariann Wasser, Susan Withers. And to those who provided meals: Countess Cawdor, Cynthia Drayton, David Sassoon, Kenneth and Carol Sharon, and Mary and Bruce Southworth.

Thanks to the curators of historic houses, especially Jim Abbott at Boscobel, Kathleen Eagen Johnson at Montgomery Place, Christine Meadows at Mount Vernon, Meg Haley of Old Sturbridge Village, and Mrs. J. Van Ness Philip of Talavera.

Thanks to the many magazines who were generous in sharing photographs, especially Betty Boote of *House Beautiful*, and Deborah Gresty and Nadine Bertin of *British House & Garden*.

Thanks as well to our spouses: to Albert Douglas, Murray's husband and a neat wordsmith himself for making text suggestions. And to Keith, Emma, and Jassy Irvine, and Chippy's animals, for putting up with our absences and distraction.

Most of all, thanks to the many talented designers who submitted work or had their work photographed — a very time-consuming process — many of which sadly have had to be lost on the cutting room floor. We would have loved to have included everyone's rooms, but there is a limit on pictures. We held onto too many too long in the hope of including them.

As coauthors, when we began this book neither of us had any idea how we would weather the association. Happily, despite long hours spent together, we have never had a serious disagreement. What's more, now that the book is completed, we miss each other!

Index to Names & Photograph Credits ❧

Photograph Credits

(B = bottom; BL = bottom
left; BR = bottom right;
I = inset; IT = inset top;
IB = inset bottom; L = left;
M = middle; R = right;
T = top; TR = top right;
TL = top left)

Jaime Ardiles-Arce, 103, 173L
ARS Limited, 82
Ernest Beadle, 104B
Gordon Beall, viIB, 142R, 150R
Fernando Bengoechea, 139
Nicholas Bryant, 152B
Edgar and Remi Clark, 166
Billy Cunningham, 5, 132T, 175
Michal Daniel, 110R
Edgar de Evia, 125
Robert Dion, 54
Jacques Dirand, 15
Scott Dressell-Martin, 110
Michael Dunne, 95, 132B
Phillip H. Ennis, 126, 153T, 159
Feliciano, 13
Eric Figge, 112
Martin Fine, 97B
Scott Frances, 60
Oberto Gili, 119T
Kari Haavisto, 83, 143
Mick Hales, 121
Alec Hemer, 4
Horst, 6, 96
Koch Studio, Inc., 155B
Dennis Krukowski, 27, 130T
Erik Kvalsvick, 85
Daniel Langley, 165
Kit Latham, 162T
Chung Lee, 173R
Tim Lee, 114
Richard Levy, 87
Guy Lindsay, 155T
Dave Marlow, 108
Carl Maupin, 90
Robert McLaughlin, 168B
Alex McLean, i, iii, v, viIT, vii,
   x–xi, 7, 8, 9, 14, 18L, 19, 22,
   23I, 26, 28B, 36, 42, 45, 49,
   50, 52, 53, 57, 58, 59, 61, 62,
   63, 66, 69, 75R, 78, 79TL,
   86, 91, 92, 93, 94, 98, 99I,
   101, 104T, 105, 107T, 109,
   111T, 113, 116, 118R, 120,
   122T, 123, 128IB, 129, 130B,
   131TL, 137, 142L, 144, 148,
   149, 150L, 154, 160T, 161T,
   162M and B, 163, 164, 167,
   168T, 169, 171, 172B, 179,
   183, 190
Melabee M Miller, 134

Michael Mundy Photographer,
   Inc., 110L
Milroy & McAleer, 99R, 145
Mary E. Nichols, 151B
Karen Radkai, 117
Stephen Randazzo, 56
Terry Richardson, 18R
Eric Roth, 16BR, 100, 151T,
   153B
Bill Rothschild, 128T
Royal Oak Showhouse, 130
Barry Rustin, 147
H. Durston Saylor, 119B, 140
David Schilling Photography,
   79BR
Keith Scott Morton, 122B
Judith Straeten, 16TL, 20, 23R,
   24, 48, 77
William P. Steele, 102
Oscar Thompson, 106
John Vaughn, 25, 174
Steve Vierra, 111B
Peter Vitale, xii, 10, 11, 88–89,
   97T, 133, 136, 172T
Clive Webster, 124T
Dennis Wilcut, 107B
Tom Yee, 152T
Eric Zepeda, 124B

For permission to reproduce
photographs in this book, the
authors also thank the
following:

ANA Hotel, Washington,
   D.C., 167
Architectural Digest. Copyright
   © 1994 by Conde Nast
   Publications, Inc. All rights
   reserved, 11, 132
Brunschwig & Fils Archives,
   20, 34, 39, 41, 72, 73, 74, 75,
   77, 84
Château de
   Thoiry-en-Yvelines, 77L
Colección Thyssen-Bornemisza,
   Madrid. Fundación
   Colección Thyssen-
   Bornemisza, Madrid. All
   rights reserved, 3
Colonial Homes, 121 and back
   jacket
Conde Nast Publications, Inc.,
   6, from *Billy Baldwin
   Decorates* by Billy Baldwin,
   1972
Connaissance des Arts, 26
Linda Floyd, designer, 25
Four Seasons Hotel, 173
Gracie Mansion Conservancy,
   60

Harvard Faculty Club, 171
Hickory Chair Co., The Mount
   Vernon Collection, 85
Historic Hudson Valley, 61
House & Garden. Copyright ©
   1984, 1969, 1989, 1992, 1985
   by Conde Nast Publications,
   Inc. All rights reserved, 6,
   13, 104B, 119T, 122B, 125
House Beautiful. Copyright ©
   1989, 1987, 1989, 1993, 1985
   by The Hearst Corporation,
   5, 102, 117, 143, 152
The Inn at Depot Hill, Capitola
   by the Sea, California, 25,
   174
Jonathan Club Restaurant, 70
Kips Bay Photo Archives, 118L
Lindy Lieberman, 131BR
Maison Prelle, 17
Montgomery Place, 61
Mount Vernon Ladies
   Association, 15
Musée du Papier Peint, 75L
National Historical Museum,
   Moscow, 82
New Albany Country Club,
   New Albany, Ohio, 175
Old Sturbridge Village, 64
Dennis Rolland, Inc., 118
Royal Oak Showhouse, 130
The Royal Pavilion Art Gallery
   and Museums, Brighton, 73B
John Rutledge House Inn, 169
Texeira, Inc., 173
Winterthur Museum. All rights
   reserved, 21

Library of Congress
Cataloging-in-Publication Data

Douglas, Murray.
   Brunschwig style / Murray
Douglas and Chippy Irvine. —
1st ed.
   p.   cm.
   "A Bulfinch Press book."
   Includes bibliographical
references and index.
   ISBN 0-8212-2041-1
   1. Brunschwig et fils.
2. Textile fabrics in interior
decoration.   3. Textile fabrics
— History — 20th century.
4. Wall coverings — History
— 20th century.   I. Irvine,
Chippy.   II. Title.
NK8998.B76D68   1994
747.213 — dc20   94-40231

DESIGNED BY SUSAN MARSH ⚘ COMPOSITION BY DIX TYPE ⚘ PRINTED AND BOUND BY TIEN WAH PRESS